# EVERYDAY WORDS
## From Names
## of People
## & Places

*Also by Allan Wolk*

The Naming of America
The Presidency and Black Civil Rights:
Eisenhower to Nixon

# Allan Wolk, Ph.D.

# EVERYDAY WORDS

# From Names of People of People & Places

ELSEVIER/NELSON BOOKS
*New York*

Library of Congress Cataloging in Publication Data

Wolk, Allan, 1936–
Everyday words from names of people and places.

1. English language—Etymology—Glossaries,
vocabularies, etc.   2. English language—Eponyms—
Glossaries, vocabularies, etc.   3. Names, English.
I. Title.
PE1583.W6   1979        422        79–26768
ISBN 0–525–66674–5

Published in the United States by Elsevier/Nelson Books,
a division of Elsevier-Dutton Publishing Company, Inc.,
New York. Published simultaneously in Don Mills,
Ontario, by Nelson/Canada.

Printed in the U.S.A.   First Edition

10   9   8   7   6   5   4   3   2   1

# Acknowledgments

In early spring 1977, Ann Finlayson, an editor friend, gave me the idea and some seed words for what eventually turned out to be this book. Many thanks, Ann.

A good deal of the two years of research was done in the Nanuet, New York, public library, an enjoyable place to work. It was made so by the friendly helpfulness of its competent staff, to whom warm thanks are also due.

Can I ever say enough to a family that had to do without a husband and a father for the thousands of hours this labor of love took? I love them all the more for their patience and understanding—Iris, my wife, and Michèle, Glenn, and Brian, my children.

New City, New York
A.W.

To Mom and Dad—
A wonderful source of strength,
inspiration and . . . love

# Contents

# Introduction

"Sticks and stones can break my bones but names will never hurt me!" Not true! Those little groupings of letters can and often do have a great effect upon us. They can hurt, and they can help.

But this book is not a treatise on the power of words. It is a peek at one family of words that live within the English language—those that come from the names of people and places. Each word has its own story to tell of its roots and evolutionary journey.

The chapters within this book illustrate the broad nature of proper nouns that have become common words. They describe every aspect of life on our planet: the animal, vegetable, and mineral kingdoms; the minds and bodies of humans; our many needs—and the many activities of people as reflected in our diversity, closeness, progressive innovations, and belligerence.

They come from many sources, but perhaps literature, the Bible, and mythology are the most fruitful.

All literature is a rich source for name words, but a disproportionately large contribution has been made by such giants as William Shakespeare (*Romeo, Juliet, Falstaffian*) and Charles Dickens (*fagin, micawber, scrooge, pecksniffian*).

The Bible, as the most widely read book in the world, is naturally a great source of such words, too, among them *Judas, Cain, jezebel, jonah,* and *sodomite.* The word *Bible* itself derives from the Greek word for "book," but the Greeks in turn obtained their term from the Phoenician port of Byblos, from which papyrus—the material used to write books—was exported all over the known world.

From the third great source of such words, Greek and Roman mythology, we obtain *echo, fauna, flora, hygiene, atlas, Venus, jovial, sphinx,* and countless others. Freud incorporated a number of classical words—*oedipus, Electra, Eros, narcissism*—into his psychological theories.

11

Many names differ greatly from their original meaning. *Dunce,* for example, was derived from the name of a brilliant thirteenth-century scholastic theologian, John Duns Scotus, whose followers were derisively called Dunsmen. *Canary* has its origin in the Spanish word for "dog"—many of whom inhabited the Canary Islands. *Panties* came from the name of a holy man, Saint Pantaleon, the patron saint of physicians. And, in the same category, *bloomers* was originally the name given to a feminist outfit worn by Mrs. Amelia Jenks Bloomer.

Some eponyms immortalize men without complimenting them: *guillotine* for Dr. Joseph I. Guillotin, its humane promoter; *Bismarck herring* for the Iron Chancellor of Germany, Prince Otto von Bismarck; *nicotine* for the diplomat who extolled the virtues of the tobacco plant, Jean Nicot; and *Virginia cowslip,* a plant honoring Elizabeth I, the Virgin Queen of England.

Many words came into being by way of "mistaken identity." It was erroneously thought, for example, that *gypsies* came from Egypt (instead of India and Persia) and that the *Pennsylvania Dutch* came from Holland (instead of Germany and Switzerland). Similar mistakes were made in naming the *guinea pig* and the *turkey,* animals that really did not come from the countries whose names they bear.

We can learn a good deal from eponymous words. Let us enjoy them and profit from the tales they tell.

# Part 1

## THE KINGDOMS OF NATURE

# •1•

# The Animal Kingdom

*Fauna,* the generic term for animal life derives from the Roman goddess associated with the fauns—merry little spirits of the forests and fields, half-goat and half-man.

## HUMANS . . .

### Cro-Magnon man

A tall, erect form of early man with deep-set eyes, named for the Cro-Magnon cave near Les Eyzies, Dordogne, France, where four skeletons were found in 1868. Cro-Magnon man is considered to be the closest in body structure to modern man of all the so-called cavemen. The ancestor of modern-day Europeans, he is thought to have reached Europe some 30,000 to 40,000 years ago.

### Darwinism

The theory that species of animal life (groups of animals having common attributes and able to interbreed) evolved through natural selection, the stronger ones surviving and the weaker petering out, named for naturalist Charles Darwin (1809–1882), who first thought it out. The theory was announced to the public in Darwin's famous *On the Origin of Species.*

Darwinism, which maintained that man evolved, like any other animal, from an apelike ancestor, aroused a storm of controversy, prompting Disraeli's famous comment: "Is man an ape or an angel? Now I am on the side of the angels."

## Java man

A type of prehistoric primate, somewhat between an ape and a man, named for Java, Indonesia, where it was found in 1891. A skull cap and thighbone, unearthed by Dutch anthropologist Eugène Dubois, are believed to be 500,000 to 1 million years old.

## Neanderthal man

A prehistoric species of man with heavy brow ridge, receding chin, and sloping forehead, named for the valley of the Neander River, near Düsseldorf, West Germany, where it was found in 1856.

# PRIMATES

## Capuchin monkey

A small, wizened monkey of South America, named for the Capuchin friars because its hair peaks up on its head like a cowl. Playful and intelligent, equipped with a prehensile tail (only Latin American monkeys have prehensile tails), the capuchin is most familiar as the organ grinder's monkey.

## Diana monkey

An attractive, white-bearded guenon of western Africa, named Diana by Linnaeus because of a white crescent on its forehead, reminiscent of the Roman moon goddess.

## gorilla

The greatest of the great apes, whose name is derived from an African tribe of hairy men called Gorillas.

Together with the chimpanzee, the orangutan, and the gibbon, the gorilla is the nearest living relative to man. This shy vegetarian, which weighs a mere four or five pounds at birth but can top out at six hundred, lives only in the Central African rain forests.

## mangabey

A slender, long-tailed monkey of west-central Africa, named for Mangaby, a region in the island of Madagascar. Actually, mangabeys are never found on Madagascar, and the name results from a mistake of some early naturalist.

## monkey

A long-tailed primate of numerous genera and species, possibly named for Moneke, the ape's son in the medieval fable *Reynard the Fox*.

## Rhesus monkey

A brownish macaque of northern India, named for a mythological king of Thrace.

The rhesus is considered a sacred animal by the Hindus, who allow it to roam freely throughout temples, orchards, and gardens. In other parts of the world, especially the United States, its earthly fate is more mundane. Here it is widely used in medical research. The Rh factor is named for the rhesus monkey, in whom it was first detected.

# MAN'S BEST FRIEND: DOGS

The dog was probably the first animal domesticated by man, some fifty thousand years ago. It is, in reality, a housebroken wolf.

The dog family goes back 45 million years, and today, throughout the world, there are at least 150 million dogs in four hundred distinct breeds. These range from the 200-pound Saint Bernard to the 1½ pound Chihuahua.

## Afghan hound

A slender, long-legged, long-haired hound of the greyhound group, named Afghan because it was originally developed in the hill country of Afghanistan.

The Afghan is one of the world's oldest breeds of dog, mentioned in an Egyptian papyrus of 3000 B.C. It hunts by coursing—that is, fixing its prey by sight rather than smell and then running it down. Today its long legs, silky hair, and lean good looks make it a popular pet.

## Airedale

An English terrier named for the valley of the Aire River in Yorkshire, England. All terriers spring from breeds bred for digging up badgers, ferrets, and other ground-dwelling game. The name "terrier" comes from *terra,* Latin for "earth."

## Bedlington terrier

A lamblike dog named for the coal-mining town of Bedlington, England, in the 1820's because the local miners thought highly of its abilities as a ratter.

## Chihuahua

The world's smallest dog, originally bred by the Aztecs, and named for the state of Chihuahua, in northern Mexico. Chihuahuas average four to six inches in length and one to six pounds in weight.

## Clumber spaniel

The "aristocrat of the spaniels," named for Clumber Park in Nottingham, England, the country estate of the duke of Newcastle, where it was originally bred.

## Dalmatian

A medium-sized dog with a distinctive black-spotted white coat, named for the coastal region of Yugoslavia, Dalmatia, where it was first distinguished as a breed.

In America we know this breed as firehouse dogs, but in England they are called coach dogs, because they guarded mail coaches and accompanied fancy carriages. Their history is older than that, however, for archaeologists have unearthed paintings of spotted dogs following Egyptian chariots.

## Dandie Dinmont

A small, rough-coated terrier, used in Scotland for hunting, named for a character in Sir Walter Scott's novel *Guy Mannering*. The fictional Dandie Dinmont owned two such dogs.

## Doberman pinscher

A short-haired, medium-sized powerful dog, named for the German dog breeder who developed it about 1890, Ludwig Dobermann. *Pinscher* is the German word for "terrier," but most Dobermans are used as guard dogs.

Dobermann bred his dog by mixing several different breeds, and the result is one of the few varieties of animal named for a person.

## King Charles spaniel

A black-and-tan toy spaniel named for Charles II of England (1630–1685), who favored the breed. Once, when approached by a group of courtiers desiring a grant of land in America, he wished to mock their pretensions to religious motives. He held up one of his pets for them to see and said, "Good friends, here is a model of piety and sincerity which it might be wholesome for you to copy."

## Saint Bernard

A large, powerful breed with a keen sense of smell, named for the alpine hospice founded by Saint Bernard of Menthon in A.D. 923, where the Saint Bernards were first developed.

Bred for their ability to guide the monks through the snow, Saint Bernards have been trained for centuries to help rescue travelers through the Great Saint Bernard Pass in Switzerland. It is estimated that over the years these dogs have saved the lives of some 2,500 human beings.

## Sealyham terrier

A game, short-legged Scottielike dog, named for the town of Sealyham, Wales, near which it was developed. Captain John Edwards, who bred the first Sealyhams, had such exacting standards that any puppy not meeting them was immediately killed.

## spaniel

A droopy-eared dog with short legs, bred for retrieving game and named for its land of origin, Spain.

## Staffordshire terrier

A cross between a bulldog and an English terrier, named for the county of Staffordshire, where it was very popular in the nineteenth century. Staffordshires were often used for the "sport" of dogfighting.

# CATS . . .

Cats, domesticated five thousand years ago, greatly outnumber dogs. In the United States alone this household pet exceeds 30 million.

Through the ages cats have often received unusual treatment from society. The Egyptians deified them, even going as far as having a cat goddess of moonlight, fertility, wisdom, and hunting—Bast. In ancient Egypt the death penalty could be invoked for anyone who killed a cat. An entire household went into mourning when its sacred pet died, and its body was mummified.

The Romans prohibited all animals, except the cat, from entering their temples.

On the other hand, during the Middle Ages, the cat was thought to be in cahoots with the devil and thus was hated and feared. It was often severely punished, put on trial with owners who were accused of witchery, tortured and burned alive, drowned, or put into building foundations.

Some of the breeds named for places are Abyssinian, American shorthair, Angora, Balinese, British blue, Burmese, Havana brown, Himalayan, Maltese, Manx, Persian, Russian blue, Siamese.

## Bengal tiger

A short-haired tiger native to India and named for the province of Bengal (now Bangladesh). Though slightly smaller than its thicker-furred, lighter-colored cousin, the Siberian tiger, the Indian animal is so magnificent that it is sometimes called the royal Bengal.

## Kaffir cat

The common wild cat of the African continent, known from Egypt to the Cape of Good Hope but named after a Bantu-speaking people of South Africa. The Kaffir cat was domesticated by the Egyptians and is considered one of the ancestors of today's house pet.

## Pallas' cat

A small wildcat native to Tibet, Mongolia, and Siberia and named for German naturalist Peter S. Pallas (1741–1811), who first brought back a specimen to the West.

Pallas also gave his name to a cormorant, a sand grouse, and a kind of meteorite. ·

# HORSES . . .

Both kings and commoners had need for horses—for transportation, as load bearers, for their milk and meat, in warfare, and to till the soil. Today there are more than 250 breeds of this equine wonder, whose total number exceeds 65 million.

## cayuse

An American range pony named for the Cayuse Indians of Oregon.

## jennet

A small Spanish breed of horse named for the Zeneti, a Berber tribe famous for its expertise with horses.

## Morgan

A classic American breed of saddle and trotting horses, named for the Vermont schoolteacher who owned the progenitor, Justin Morgan (1747–1798).

## Narragansett pacer

A small, swift saddle horse, named for the Narragansett region of Rhode Island, where it was bred. Fast, tireless, famed for every virtue except looks, this animal's natural gait was the pace—moving both legs on one side at the same time—which made him comfortable to ride as well.

Deacon Larkin's mare, which carried Paul Revere on his famous ride, was probably a Narragansett pacer. Reported one colonial owner of his own lively pacer, "He always plays and acts and never will stand still. He will take a glass of wine, beer, or cyder."

## Percheron

A heavy breed of draft horse, named for the district of Percher near Normandy in northern France, where it was developed.

## Przhevalski's horse

A small, large-headed wild horse, discovered on the plains of Central Asia in 1888 and named for Russian explorer Nikolai Przhevalski. This strange animal, considered to lie halfway between the domesticated horse and the ass, is the only true wild horse in the world. The mustangs of the American West and other so-called wild herds are the descendants of once-domesticated beasts that have escaped.

## Shetland pony

The tiniest of all the pony breeds is named for the Scottish islands of Shetland and Orkney, where it originated. A child's delight, this miniature animal grows thirty-seven to forty inches high, and weighs approximately 350 pounds.

# CATTLE . . .

The Norsemen, around A.D. 1000, were the first of a number of explorers who brought cattle to America. Columbus, on his second voyage in 1493, also deposited a similar load.

Since those days the world's supply has multiplied, zooming to at least 1 billion head today. India has the greatest number, totaling well over 200 million. Most of their cattle are used only for milk and draft purposes, because of the slaughter prohibitions of the Hindu religion. The United States ranks second.

The people of the world depend on these large animals for 50 percent of their meat, 95 percent of their milk, and 80 percent of their leather goods.

## Devon

A reddish, dual-purpose (meat and milk) breed of cattle, named for the county of Devon, England, where they were developed.

## Guernsey

Brown-and-white dairy cattle, named for its place of origin, the Channel Isle (British) of Guernsey.

## Hereford

White-faced reddish-brown beef cattle, named for Herefordshire, England, where it was developed. Herefords are now the most common American meat steers.

## Holstein

Large black-and-white dairy cattle, which originated in Friesland, the Netherlands, but were later imported into Schleswig-Holstein, West Germany, and named for the latter. Known throughout the world for their copious yield of low-fat milk, these cows are called Holsteins in America and Friesian in other countries.

## Jersey

Fawn-colored dairy cattle named for Jersey, the largest of the Channel Islands, where they were bred. Jerseys are famous for the richness of their milk, high in butter fat.

## Kerry

Black, small dairy cattle named for the mountainous region of County Kerry, Eire, where they originated.

# SHEEP . . .

Sheep were one of the first animals to be domesticated, some eight thousand years ago. Of all livestock, these placid creatures have the greatest number and variety of breeds, totaling almost one thousand. There are more than 1 billion head of sheep in the world today, with Australia, the Soviet Union, and New Zealand having the largest amounts, respectively.

One sheared sheep nets from four to fifteen pounds of wool.

## Barbary sheep (aoudad)

A tawny-coated wild sheep, named for the Barbary region of North Africa, where it is found. Rams sport a distinctive beardlike growth of hair on throat and chest.

## Dorset Horn

Curly-horned sheep, fine yielders of mutton, named for Dorsetshire, England.

## Karakul

Sheep first bred near Lake Karakul, in Tadzhik, Soviet Union, and named for it. The older the animal grows, the coarser its fine, glossy wool coat becomes, so lambs are killed when they are between one week and ten days old. This ensures that the pelts will be at their curliest, glossiest best and suitable for making coats of what we call Persian lamb.

## Leicester

A sheep with long, coarse wool, first bred by Robert Bakewell, famed eighteenth-century agriculturalist, at his estate Dishley, Leicestershire, and named for the county.

## merino

A breed of sheep, producers of some of the world's finest wool, which was introduced into Spain by the Moors, probably named for the Berber tribe Beni Merin, which developed it.

Merinos were so highly prized that the Spanish government once imposed the death penalty on anyone caught exporting them. However, they have since been spread around the world, and today Australia is the chief producer of merino wool.

## Rambouillet

A fine-wool sheep named for the French national breeding station, Rambouillet, near Paris, where it was developed in the 1780's and 1790's. Later imported into the United States and subjected to further breeding experiments, Rambouillets have become the most common American sheep.

## Romney

A sheep with long, coarse wool, bred in Kent, England, and named for the coastal pastureland known as Romney Marsh.

## Targhee

An American breed of hardy, mutton-producing sheep developed at the federal government experiment station at Dubois, Idaho, in the 1920's and named for the nearby Targhee Pass between Idaho and Montana.

## Wiltshire horn

Pure-white, curly-horned sheep named for the county of Wiltshire, England, where they originated.

# GOATS . . .

Many people depend on the more than two hundred different goat breeds for milk, meat, or fleece. The United States alone imports more than 40 million goatskins a year.

## Angora goat

A variety of goat distinguished by its silky fleece and named Angora (a corruption of Ankara) from the mistaken view that it originated in the Middle East. Actually Angoras evolved in Tibet.

If the Angora is not sheared in the spring, its fleece is shed naturally during the summer. Another name for this fine wool is mohair.

## Cashmere goat

A variety of goat that yields an extremely fine grade of wool, named for the Vale of Kashmir in the Himalayas, where it originated. The wool comes from the animal's undercoat of down and is removed by combing.

# PIGS . . .

There are more than one hundred major breeds of pigs, one of the most intelligent of domesticated animals. Communist China has more swine than any other country, 25 percent of the world's 700 million.

The pig was first domesticated in China more than seven thousand years ago. It was brought to America by Columbus and other explorers.

## Chester White

A white pig named for Chester County, Pennsylvania, where it was developed.

## Duroc

A reddish-colored American breed of swine, developed in New Jersey and named Duroc for a favorite horse owned by the developer.

# OTHER ASSORTED MAMMALS

The 4,500 species of mammal living today range from the tiny shrew to the 115-foot blue whale.

## Bactrian camel

The common two-hump camel, named for a barren mountain region in central Asia where it was supposed to have originated. Ancient Bactria is now partly in Afghanistan, partly in the U.S.S.R.

The name "Bactrian camel" is used to distinguish the animal from the one-hump dromedary.

## Kodiak bear

The largest of the land carnivores, named for its habitat, Kodiak Island, off the coast of the Alaska Peninsula. Some Kodiaks have been known to stand nine feet tall when erect and to weigh over 1,600 pounds.

## Père David's deer

A strangely antlered deer, named for Father Armand David (1826–1900), a French missionary, who spied these deer in the gardens of the Summer Palace of the Chinese emperors in Peking. The emperor's herd had lived so long in captivity that no one could remember where they came from originally, and no specimen has ever been found in the wild, so the animal remains a mystery deer. It is found only in zoos today. Some males of the species shed and grow two sets of antlers per year.

Father David's name is also borne by a cliff-dwelling squirrel found in South China.

## Steller's sea cow

A large vegetarian sea mammal, named for naturalist Georg Wilhelm Steller (1709–1746), who discovered it in 1741 off the coast of the Komandorski Islands. Within twenty-seven years the animal was extinct, slaughtered by seal hunters for food.

Steller, who accompanied Vitus Bering on two exploration trips to the Kamchatka and Alaska coastal areas, has also given his name to a sea eagle, an eider duck, a jay, and a sea lion.

## Tasmanian devil

A burrowing, meat-eating marsupial, once widespread in Australia but now confined to the island of Tasmania and named for it.

Black, almost hairless, the creature has extremely powerful jaws with which it completely devours its prey—skin and bones. But it is far from the frightful horror depicted in some animated cartoons, for in general its life habits most closely resemble those of the raccoon. It is nearly extinct.

## Tasmanian tiger (wolf)

A marsupial (the female has a belly pouch for the young) named for its place of origin, Tasmania, Australia. It is yellow-brown with sixteen to eighteen brown bars on its back and tail, and is considered the largest living flesh-eating marsupial. It is nearly extinct.

# BIRDS . . .

Birds evolved from the reptile family, probably from some smaller type of dinosaur. They all have feathers and usually no teeth.

## Adélie penguin

One of only two species of penguin (the other is the emperor) which live on the continent of Antarctica itself, named for the Adélie Coast. These hardy birds—the Adélie Coast is considered the windiest spot on the globe, often buffeted by 200-mile-per-hour gales—trudge many miles over the ice to their nesting grounds.

## Baltimore oriole

A common American oriole named for Cecil Calvert, Lord Baltimore, because its bright orange-and-black plumage reminded early settlers of the Calvert coat of arms. The Lords Baltimore were founders and Proprietors of the colony of Maryland.

## bantam

A small chicken (under 20 ounces) named for the Bantam (now Banten) region of Java in Indonesia, where it originated.

The terms "bantam" and "bantam rooster" are used jocularly of any small, pugnacious person. A boxer fighting in the bantamweight division may not weigh more than 118 pounds.

## canary

A small golden finch named for the Canary Islands, of which it is a native, and widely domesticated as a pet songbird.

Actually this bird's name originally meant "dog." The Roman name for the islands off the West Coast of Africa (now Spanish) was *Insulae Canariae,* Dog Islands, because of the large number of canines found there. The Spanish, after they took over the islands in 1404, kept the name. Later, when men began to catch and domesticate the "Canary finch," they shortened the name to "canary."

## Dominique

An American breed of domestic fowl with barred plumage, named for its island of origin, Dominica, in the Windward Islands.

Early Americans sometimes pronounced the bird's name "Dominaker," and it occasionally appears like that in old folk songs.

## Franklin gull

A small, black-headed gull native to western North America and named for Arctic explorer Sir John Franklin. Unlike most members of their family, Franklin gulls nest inland and feed on insects, and for this reason they are credited with having saved Brigham Young's Mormon settlement at Salt Lake City.

The Mormons, after many tribulations, had managed to reach their promised land and put in a much-needed crop, only to see a horde of grasshoppers arrive and settle on their freshly planted fields. But before the insects could destroy the crops, a flock of gulls descended on them and ate the grasshoppers. In gratitude the Mormons erected a monument to the gulls and chose the gull as the state bird of Utah.

## Harlequin duck

A diving duck commonest along the coast of Northwest United States, Canada, and Alaska, named for the Commedia dell'Arte clown Harlequin. The bird's queer feather patterns and markings suggest the particolored costume always associated with Harlequin.

## Houdan

A French breed of domestic fowl with a V-shaped comb, named for the village of Houdan, near Versailles, where it was developed.

## Leghorn

A large breed of domestic poultry—twelve different varieties—belonging to the Mediterranean Class and taking its name from the Italian seaport of Leghorn (Ligurno).

Among American egg farmers, the White Leghorn is the preeminent breed, preferred for its excellent laying qualities.

## martin

A small European swallow named for Saint Martin of Tours (315–397) because it migrates from England around Martinmas (November 11).

Saint Martin, born in what is now Hungary, was serving in the Roman army when he was approached by a naked beggar, to whom he gave half his cloak. That night in a dream Jesus appeared to him, wearing the half cloak, and said, "Martin covered me with this garment." And this led to his becoming a Christian, a bishop, and a great early missionary.

## Mother Carey's chicken

The most familiar and wide-ranging of the storm (or stormy) petrels, which takes this nickname from the medieval sailor's prayer to *Mater Cara* ("dear Mother"), an epithet of the Virgin Mary.

The term "stormy petrel" is often applied to a human troublemaker.

## Orpington

A chunky-built breed of poultry belonging to the English Class and named for Orpington, Kent, where it was developed. Orpingtons come in four color varieties—buff, white, black, and blue—and are more popular in England and Australia than in the United States. Orpingtons are raised either as meat producers or for both meat and eggs.

## petrel

A type of small, long-winged sea bird that flies far from land to feed and is thought to be named for Saint Peter:

> And when Peter was come down out of the ship,
> he walked on the water, to go to Jesus.
>
> (Matthew 14:29)

## pheasant

A wild game bird, related to the domestic chicken and named by the Greeks *phasianos ornis* ("Phasian bird"), from the River Phasis in Colchis (now the Rion River in Soviet Georgia).

The pheasant is not native to America, but in the 1880's sportsmen introduced the Chinese ring-necked pheasant to this country, and it made itself at home so quickly that it is now found from Oregon to New York and from Baja California to British Columbia.

The *argus pheasant* is a big bird with numerous brightly colored spots on its tail that look like eyes. In Greek mythology the hundred eyes of the monster Argus were bequeathed to the tail of a peacock, but here they adorn the plumage of the peacock's close relative.

Someone who is "argus-eyed" is vigilant or observant.

## Plymouth Rock

A medium-sized, long-legged breed of poultry, belonging to the American Class and named for the Pilgrims' landing site in the New World. Plymouth Rocks, most popular in barred and white varieties, are raised chiefly as broilers and fryers.

## Rhode Island Red and White

Two color varieties of a popular breed of domestic poultry, belonging to the American Class and named for the area where they originated. (All American poultry breeding had its beginnings in New England.) Both Rhode Island Reds, which sport a rich bronze plumage, and Whites are bred chiefly as laying hens, but Reds are also good meat producers.

## serin

A small European finch, related to the canary and named for those mythological songstresses, the Sirens. The Sirens were sweet-singing creatures, half woman and half bird, who lured sailors toward them to be crushed on the rocks of the shore.

## Tragopan

A genus of Asiatic pheasants which takes its name from the Greek word *tragopan* ("goat of Pan"), because of the hornlike extensions on the head of the male. In Greek mythology, Pan was, among other things, the god of woods and flocks and sported a goat's ears, hind legs, hooves, and horns.

## turkey

A large domestic fowl, developed from a native American wild game bird and named for what was mistakenly thought to be its country of origin.

Europeans confused the American turkey with the guinea fowl, a bird native to Africa and Madagascar, which had been introduced to Europe by way of Turkey and was known to the Spanish and Portuguese as "the turkey." This confusion was helped along by the American bird's magnificent bronze-and-red iridescent plumage, for Europeans thought of brilliant colors as typically Near Eastern.

Turkeys are nearly extinct in the wild, but the domestic breeds are on the increase, and production reaches 100 million birds annually. Mount Tom, near Northampton, Massachusetts, was named for an elusive old gobbler who lived there for many years.

# REPTILES . . .

Reptiles were the first vertebrates that established themselves as permanent dwellers on land. For some 160 million years they were the dominant life form on the earth; then, some 80 million years ago, they began to lose ground, until today they are known from only four orders: crocodilians, turtles, lizards, and snakes.

## Aesculapius' snake

A small black rat snake of Europe, harmless to humans, and named for Aesculapius, the Greek-Roman god of medicine, because it is thought to be the species kept by Romans in his temples. It is represented on the Staff of Aesculapius, a winged stick with a snake entwined around it, which is the international symbol of physicians.

## Gaboon viper

The largest of the vipers, extremely poisonous, named for the Gabon region of West Africa, where it is commonly found. Gaboons are beautiful snakes, brilliantly colored in black, chartreuse, mauve, and buff, and despite the extreme deadliness of their venom and the great length of their fangs (an inch and a half, longest of any viper), they are not aggressive animals. When surprised, a Gaboon flattens itself out, makes feinting jabs at the intruder, and blows loudly through its nostrils.

## Gila monster

A thick-bodied, brightly colored venomous lizard of the arid American Southwest, named for the Gila River in Arizona, where men first encountered it. The Gila (pronounced *heel-a*) is one of only two species of lizard known to be venomous, the other being its close relative, the beaded lizard of neighboring Mexico.

The Gila monster is not equipped with fangs but with crude poison grooves in its jaws, and when it has bitten someone, it must chew in order to pump up the venom from the glands that contain it. Therefore, if the victim instantly flings the lizard away—not easy to do, for it bites deep and hangs on for dear life—he may escape being poisoned.

## Komodo dragon

A monitor lizard, the largest lizard in the world, named for the Indonesian island of Komodo, where it was first found. Oddly enough, this ten-foot-long monitor was unknown to the Western world until 1912, when a Dutch naturalist, P. A. Ouwens, obtained a specimen.

## Massasauga rattlesnake

A small ground rattler, frequenting swampy regions, and named for Missisauga River, in Ontario, near which it was first identified.

## Nile crocodile

The common crocodile of the African continent, first encountered by Westerners in the Egyptian Nile and therefore named for it. A powerful and savage beast, feared by native hunters and zookeepers alike, the Nile crocodile is considered to be the most dangerous creature in Africa. Nevertheless, some native Africans do hunt it successfully and use the plated hide as armor. It is arrow-proof.

## Python

A genus of nonvenomous, constricting snakes, named for the mythical serpent that haunted the caves of Parnassus and was slain by Apollo. Thereafter the god set up his oracle at nearby Delphi and spoke prophecies through the priestess, called Pythia.

Pythons are the world's longest and largest snakes and have been known to devour small goats, pigs, deer, and other mammals. One huge python in Malaya is said to have devoured a fourteen-year-old boy.

The Indian python, as pythons go, is relatively docile and is a favorite "snake-charming" snake. Well cared for, circus snakes may live for years.

# CREATURES OF THE SEA . . .

Fish, constituting 30,000 species, are the most numerous of all vertebrates. This 500-million-year-old class yields an annual world catch of 150 billion tons.

## bocaccio

A Pacific Ocean rockfish called *bocacha* ("big mouth") by Latin Americans, which name has been corrupted by common speech to bocaccio—perhaps in honor of fourteenth-century Italian writer Giovanni Boccaccio (1313–1375).

## Chinook salmon

The largest species of American salmon (also called king salmon), found in Pacific waters north of Monterey and named for the Chinook Indians, who were great salmon fishermen. The Chinooks had several well-established salmon-fishing sites at the cascades and falls of the Columbia and Willamette rivers, where they gathered every year for the spawning run.

A chinook wind is a warm breeze—in cold regions, the spring wind that melts the winter snow.

## daphnia

A primitive freshwater crustacean, very tiny, named for the Greek nymph Daphne. Fleeing from the embraces of Apollo, Daphne called on her father, the river god Peneus, for aid, and he responded by changing her into a laurel tree.

Daphnia form an important source of aquarium food.

## Dolly Varden

A large, colorfully spotted Western trout, named for Dolly Varden, an overdressed coquette in Charles Dickens' *Barnaby Rudge*.

Trout are normally freshwater fish, but like some species of rainbow trout (called steelheads), Dolly Vardens may spend part of their lives at sea, returning to fresh water to spawn.

## garibaldi

A tropical marine fish of the California coast, brilliant orange-red in color, named for Italian liberator Giuseppe Garibaldi (1807–1882). Garibaldi's troops were distinguished by the bright red shirts they wore.

## guppy

A small Barbadian minnow, named for R.J.L. Guppy of Trinidad, who discovered and first brought it into England. Guppies are now popular home-aquarium fish.

## molly

A tropical minnow named for Comte François Nicholas Mollien (1758–1850), Napoleon's minister of finance.

## Oquassa trout

A small trout found only in the Rangeley chain of lakes in northwestern Maine and named for Oquossoc, a town on the strait between Rangeley and Mooselookmeguntic lakes.

## Pismo clam

A thick-shelled clam of the California coast, named for Pismo Beach, about 140 miles north of Los Angeles. Pismos, widely used for food, live an average of eight years, although on occasion they have survived for up to twenty-five years.

## Portuguese man-of-war

A tropical sea organism (but often carried as far north as New England) called Portuguese apparently because of its beautiful colors and man-of-war because of the damage it can do to an unwary swimmer who encounters it.

This siphonophore is not one animal but a colony of them, consisting of a balloonlike bladder, which the colony can deflate or inflate (with a self-generated gas) at will, and a trail of tentacles containing stinging cells. These tentacles, which can be shortened or lengthened to as much as forty feet, are the animal's means of obtaining food, for its sting can easily kill small fish—and inflict a nasty welt on human flesh, too. The iridescent bladder is the colony's "sail" and is often encountered far out to sea, being carried before the wind.

## Saint Peter's fish

A deep-living marine fish (also called a John dory) with a dark spot on either side of its mouth, named for the Apostle Peter. There is a legend that this is the fish from whose mouth Saint Peter obtained a coin to pay a tax that was due, as Jesus ordered him:

> Go thou to the sea, and cast an hook, and take up the fish that first cometh up; and when thou hast opened his mouth, thou shalt find a piece of money: that take, and give unto them for me and thee. (Matthew 17:27)

## Triton

A marine mollusk with a conical shell, named for the sea divinity Triton, who blows a similar-shaped shell to create waves or calm the sea.

Triton, son of Poseidon and Amphitrite, is usually depicted with the tail of a dolphin and the head and body of a man—and sometimes also the front legs of a horse.

## Venus's-flower-basket

A sandy sponge that looks like glassy intricate lace or spun glass when the animal is dried out, named for the Roman goddess of love and beauty.

## Venus's-girdle

A five-foot marine animal with a ribbonlike iridescent body, named for the goddess Venus.

# INSECTS . . .

Insects have evolved to their present state over a period of 400 million years. As picnickers will readily confirm, they are the most widespread of all animals, constituting more than a million different species. Their phenomenal diversity ranges from tiny fairy flies—1/100th of an inch long—to giant moths with ten-inch wingspreads.

## Amazon ant

A genus of European and American ants, named for the nation of female warriors of Greek myth. The Amazons were reputed to carry off and raise the children of other tribes, and similarly Amazon ants kidnap the larva of other species and rear them as slaves.

The Amazon River of South America and the vast basin it waters got their name from Spanish explorers who thought they had seen female warriors along the banks.

## Goliath beetle

A genus of large African beetles, up to four inches in length, named for the Biblical giant Goliath, who was slain by David (I Samuel 17).

## Guinea worm

A threadlike parasite common to tropical Africa, which invades warm-blooded hosts by way of drinking water. It secures itself beneath the skin of human beings and other mammals and is removed by native Africans by being wound around a stick. Guinea worms can grow to a length of four feet.

## Gypsy moth

A European tussock moth, named for the Gypsies, famed wanderers of Europe. Accidentally introduced into the United States in 1869, this insect, in its caterpillar form, proved horrendously destructive to deciduous forests and ornamental trees. But the adult female seldom flies, so that, despite its name, it is not a great traveler, and this has enabled forestry experts to prevent it from spreading much beyond New England.

## Hercules beetle

A huge Central American and Caribbean beetle, four to six inches long, named for the Greek hero and strong man, Hercules. These beetles carry a "horn" on their heads that may be as long as two inches, but despite this and their own massive size (as big as a man's fist) they are capable of flying—a truly herculean feat.

## Hessian fly

A small gall midge, named Hessian because it is thought to have been introduced to the United States in the straw bedding of Hessian soldiers during the Revolution. Hessian flies are plant-eaters and extremely destructive to crops of wheat, barley, and rye.

## Io moth

A large yellow American moth with an eyelike spot on its wings, named for the Greek nymph Io.

Zeus fell in love with Io, and when Hera heard about it, he changed the girl into a heifer and, to allay his wife's suspicions, gave the animal to her. Not altogether placated, Hera set hundred-eyed Argus to watch the heifer night and day. Io mourned and prayed to Zeus to be freed from his spell, and at last he sent Hermes to lull the monster to sleep with magic music and then cut off his head. Then Io was released from the spell and returned to her own shape.

Hera, in memory of her servant, placed his eyes on the tail of her bird, the peacock. It is the similar wing spots on the Io moth that cause it to be named for this old myth.

## Jesus bug

A long-legged bug (also called a water strider) that moves on top of fresh water, named in allusion to the Biblical description of Jesus walking on water:

And in the fourth watch of the night Jesus went unto them, walking on the sea. (Matthew 14:25)

## ladybug

A small spotted beetle, a favorite with children, named for "Our Lady," an epithet of the Virgin Mary. In German these attractive creatures are called *Marienkäferchen* ("Mary beetles").

## Mexican jumping bean

Not a bean at all but a fruit seed that contains the larva of a small moth, named Mexican because it is chiefly found south of the border. When the seed is held in the hand, the movements of the larva cause it to roll and hop.

## Polyphemus moth

A large American silk moth of yellowish brown with an eyelike spot on either wing, named for the one-eyed Cyclops of the *Odyssey*.
Polyphemus imprisoned Odysseus and his men in his cave, and they escaped by blinding him and then clinging to the undersides of his sheep as he released them to go out to pasture.

## Promethea moth

A large American silk moth of reddish brown and dark red, named for the Greek hero Prometheus.
Prometheus, the champion of men against the gods, defied an order of Zeus and brought fire down from heaven for men. In punishment for this daring deed, he was chained to a rock, where an eagle tore out his liver every day. He was eventually rescued by Hercules.

The word "promethean" has always been used to express daring originality in men, and perhaps it has been applied to this moth for the same reason. When it becomes time to spin a cocoon, the caterpillar sews itself into a folded leaf and secures the leaf to its twig with strands of its own silk.

## Saint Mark's fly

A two-winged, grass-eating fly named for Saint Mark because it emerges for the season about the time of his feast day (April 25).

## Saturnia

A silk moth of the family Saturnidae, named for Saturnia ("daughter of Saturn"), an epithet for Juno.

## Spanish fly

Not a fly at all but a bright-green southern European blister beetle, named Spanish because it is most commonly found in Spain.

It was widely used at one time for the sake of the cantharis it contained. This substance was obtained from the beetle's crushed body and applied for the purpose of raising counterirritant blisters. It was also sometimes taken internally as an aphrodisiac, but this turned out to be a dangerous practice, for cantharis is toxic.

## tarantula

A large hairy spider which kills its prey by injecting it with poison and named for the town where it was originally found, Taranto, a seaport in southern Italy. Some species, especially those of tropical South America, are enormous—large enough to catch and kill small birds.

The tarantula's bite is not poisonous to man, but at one time it was believed that the victim of a tarantula bite could only save his life by flinging himself into a wild dance. In southern Italy, people still dance the tarantella.

Female tarantulas live longer than males—up to twenty years. Some species make excellent pets, learn to recognize their master (which is more than pet snakes can do), and display great intelligence.

# · 2 ·

# The Vegetable Kingdom

Our world would be as desolate and dreary as the moon without the abundant varieties of vegetation that dot the Earth.

*Flora,* the sweet-sounding word that signifies plant life, was the name of the Roman goddess of flowers and spring. The Romans celebrated the coming of this delightful season with the Floralia, a wild festival that took place from April 28 to May 3.

Many plants, especially those of North and South America, previously unknown to Europeans, were given their formal and even their common names by the Swedish taxonomist Carl von Linné, better known by the Latinized form of his name, Carolus Linnaeus.

Linnaeus, who invented the system by which we scientifically identify all life forms today, liked to honor fellow botanists, horticulturalists, and patrons of science by giving their names to newly discovered plants, even if they were not the first to locate them.

## PLANTS AND FLOWERS . . .

### Aaron's rod

A tall, straight-stemmed mullein, so called from the biblical story of Moses and the miracle of Aaron's staff:

> Moses went into the tabernacle of witness; and, behold, the rod of Aaron for the house of Levi was budded, and brought forth buds, and bloomed blossoms, and yielded almonds. (Numbers 17:8)

43

## Adam and Eve

A North American orchid (also called putty root), whose bulbs look like human beings, named for the biblical progenitors of the human race.

*Adam* is the Hebrew word for "man" or "mankind," and *Eve* means "living one."

## Apache plume

An evergreen shrub of the rose family whose fruit takes a plumelike form, named for the Apache Indians, whose ancient hunting grounds were the southwestern United States and northern Mexico, where the plant is found.

## Artemisia

A genus of strong-smelling plants, scattered worldwide and named for Artemis, the Greek goddess of the hunt. Sagebrush is the common American form of Artemisia.

## Begonia

A genus of flowering succulents, native to the tropics but widely cultivated elsewhere in gardens and as houseplants, named in honor of Michel Begon (1638–1710), French governor of Santo Domingo and a patron of science.

## boltonia

An asterlike American wildflower, common in eastern coastal regions, named for the eighteenth-century English botanist James Bolton.

## Bouvardia

A genus of dwarf shrubs named for the seventeenth-century French physician Charles Bouvard.

# bromeliad

A family of tropical American epiphytes—that is, plants that use other plants (usually trees) as plant stands but are not parasitic—named for Olaf Bromelius (1639–1705), a Swedish botanist. Our most familiar bromeliad, now grown on the ground, is the pineapple.

# Buddleia

A genus of flowering shrubs named for Adam Buddle (d. 1715), a British botanist. Buddleias are sometimes called butterfly bushes because their flowers attract these beautiful flying insects.

# Camellia

A genus of tropical Asiatic evergreen flowering shrubs, named for a Jesuit missionary to the Philippines, who first described it, Georg Josef Kamel (1661–1706).

# Canterbury bells

A garden plant named Canterbury because its bell-shaped flowers are thought to resemble the small bells on the horses of religious pilgrims traveling to the shrine of Saint Thomas of Canterbury.

Archbishop Thomas à Becket (1118–1170) was murdered by four followers of King Henry II, because of the prelate's zealous support of clerical rights, a deed that shocked all of Christendom. His shrine became one of the great attractions for pilgrims throughout the Middle Ages.

In his famous *Canterbury Tales* (published circa 1400), considered the first work of art to be produced in English, poet Geoffrey Chaucer described the various types of pilgrims who traveled to this renowned shrine.

# Cattleya

A genus of showy American orchids named for a nineteenth-century British benefactor of botany, William Cattley.

## Christ's thorn

A thorny shrub, native to Palestine, named for the crown of thorns placed on Jesus' head at the time of his crucifixion.

The *Jerusalem thorn* (no botanical relation to Christ's thorn) is a piny tropical tree found in the southern and southwestern parts of the United States.

## Clarkia

A genus of western American flowering herbs, named for William Clark (1170–1838), army officer, explorer, and the other half of the famed Lewis and Clark expedition. Clark discovered this plant during the pair's two-year trek to the Pacific Ocean.

## Claytonia

A genus of North American succulents, also known as spring beauties, and named for the English-born American botanist John Clayton (1693–1773).

## Clintonia

A genus of flowering herbs belonging to the lily family, also called the corn lily, named in honor of De Witt Clinton (1769–1828), American politician.

Clinton, a New Yorker and nephew of New York's first governor, had a long and varied political career in the Empire State. He served as assemblyman, state senator, United States Senator, mayor of New York City, lieutenant governor, and governor. He lost the 1812 Presidential election to James Madison, but is best remembered as the driving force behind the creation of the historic Erie Canal.

## Collinsia

A genus of American herbs named for Zaccheus Collins (1764–1831), an American botanist. Common names for some Collinsias are blue-eyed Mary, horse-balm, and innocence.

## Dahlia

A genus of American tuberous herbs with showy flowers, named for Anders Dahl, an eighteenth-century Swedish botanist and a pupil of Linnaeus. There are more than 2,000 varieties of this popular garden flower.

## David's-harp

A species of Solomon seal which got its name because its flowering stalk is thought to resemble the ancient type of harp that the biblical David played for King Saul:

> And it came to pass, when the evil spirit from God was upon Saul, that David took a harp, and played with his hand: so Saul was refreshed, and was well, and the evil spirit departed from him. (I Samuel 16–23)

## Deutzia

A genus of ornamental shrubs (related to the saxifrages) of Central America and Asia and named for Jean Deutz, an eighteenth-century Dutch patron of botany.

## Dutchman's breeches

An attractive American wildflower so named because its fragrant "two-legged" blossoms are thought to resemble baggy Dutch leg coverings.

## Echeveria

A genus of tropical American succulents, named for the nineteenth-century Mexican botanical illustrator, Señor Echeveria. Among the common forms of these plants are stonecrop and sedum.

## Forsythia

A genus of ornamental shrubs of Europe and Asia, named for William Forsyth (1737–1804), superintendant of the British Royal Gardens at St. James and Kensington.

Golden forsythia, blooming in earliest spring, is so popular in hard-bitten Brooklyn, New York, that it has been named the borough's official flower.

## Fuchsia

A genus of small shrubs with pendulous flowers (popular in hanging baskets), related to the evening primrose and named for the German botanist Leonhard Fuchs (1501–1566).

Originally this beautiful plant was pronounced *fewksia,* but has now been softened to *fewsha.*

## Gaillardia

A genus of western American plants with hairy foliage, named for Gaillard de Marentonneau, eighteenth-century French botanist. Common names for Gaillardia are blanketflower and Indian blanket.

## Gardenia

A genus of European and Asian tropical shrubs having extremely fragrant blossoms of white or yellow, named for Dr. Alexander Garden (1731–1791), a Scots-born American naturalist and physician.

Garden, a member of the Royal Society, emigrated to South Carolina in 1754, where he collected many specimens. He was a Loyalist during the Revolution, but his son joined the Continental Army in 1780 and served until the end of the war.

## Gentian

A genus of flowering herbs, of which more than four hundred species are known, named for Gentius, king of Illyria, conquered by the

Romans in 168 B.C. Gentius is said to have been the first to learn of the tonic qualities of these plants.

## Good-King-Henry

A European goosefoot, sometimes eaten as a potherb, named for England's first Tudor monarch, Henry VII (1457–1509).

## herb Robert

A geranium with reddish-purple flowers, probably named for the eleventh-century French abbot who became Saint Robert.

## Hyacinth

A genus of garden plants of the lily family, including the flowering hyacinth and the water hyacinth, named for the mythological youth Hyacinth, accidentally killed by the wind god Zephyrus, who caused the quoit, with which the boy was playing, to strike his head and fell him. Apollo, who loved the boy, created the flower from his spilled blood.

## Jacob's-ladder

A European wildflower whose paired leaflets are thought to resemble a ladder, named for the biblical reference to Jacob's dream:

> And he dreamed, and behold a ladder set up on the earth, and the top of it reached to heaven: and behold the angels of God ascending and descending on it. (Genesis 28:12)

## Jacob's-rod

An erect-standing flower of the lily family, named for the biblical Jacob and his peeled-poplar rod:

> And Jacob took him rods of green poplar, and of the hazel

and chesnut tree; and pilled white strakes in them, and made the white appear which was in the rods. (Genesis 30:37)

## Jerusalem artichoke

A tuberous relative of the American sunflower, whose popular name is a corruption of the Italian *girasole* ("sunflower"). Jerusalem artichokes are edible by man but are more often used as a feed for livestock.

## Jim Hill mustard

A biennial herb of European origin, often a troublesome weed in North America, named for railroad magnate James J. Hill (1836–1916), because it grew so profusely by the untended tracks.

## jimsonweed

A poisonous weed, closely related to the tomato, named Jamestown weed for the 1607 settlement where it was first encountered.

This plant, sometimes called the thorn apple, was used by ancient Mexicans to put themselves into a trancelike state, during which they thought they could identify unknown thieves. Gambling Indians of Mexico and southern California believed it brought them luck.

## jipajapa

A palmlike Central and South American plant, named for the town of Jipajapa, Ecuador, near which the plants are found. The fan-shaped leaves of this plant are used to make Panama hats.

## Joshua tree

A large treelike plant of the yucca family, with sword-shaped leaves and branches extending like arms, named for the biblical description of the Israelite military commander Joshua. Joshua was appointed by Moses to be his successor and the commander of the troops of Israel:

And the Lord said unto Joshua, Stretch out the spear that is
in thy hand toward Ai; for I will give it into thine hand. And
Joshua stretched out the spear that he had in his hand toward
the city. (Joshua 8:18)

## Lespedeza

A genus of herbaceous plants of the bean family named for Vincente
Manuel de Cespedes (the name was misread), a Spanish governor of
eastern Florida. Lespedezas provide important animal forage and hay.

## Lobelia

A genus of widespread flowering plants, named for Matthias de Lobel
(1538–1616), a Flemish botanist and the royal physician to James I of
England.

## loosestrife

A yellow-flowered plant of the primrose family whose name is a crude
translation of Lysimachus ("Deliverance from Battle"), the name of a
fourth-century B.C. Greek doctor.

## Madonna lily

A lily with white trumpet-shaped flowers, named for the Madonna,
the Virgin Mary.

## Magnolia

A genus of North American and Asiatic trees, named for the French
botanist and physician Pierre Magnol (1638–1715). The classification of
plants by families was a scientific innovation of Dr. Magnol.

## Maranta

A genus of tropical American herbs with starchy tuberous roots, named for the sixteenth-century Italian physician and herbalist Bartolomeo Maranta. The best-known plant of this genus is arrowroot, which yields a starchy substance much used in children's food and invalid diets, and in French cooking for thickening a clear sauce.

## Marigold

A genus of American flowering herbs, usually blossoming a bright yellow, named for the Virgin Mary.

## Michelia

A genus of Asiatic shrubs related to the magnolias, named for Piero Antonio Micheli, eighteenth-century Italian botanist.

## Monarda

A genus of North American mints, named for Dr. N. Monardes, a Spanish botanist, and widely used by Indians and colonists alike as headache remedies and garden plants.

## Narcissus

A genus of Old World flowering perennials, named for the handsome youth of Greek myth, Narcissus. As punishment for his egotistical conceit, he was made to gaze interminably at his beautiful image in a mountain pond, and during this period he was turned into a flower.

## Nicotiana

A genus of American and Asiatic herbs of the potato family, named for the French diplomat Jean Nicot (1530–1600), the lord of Villemain. The most famous member of this genus is smoking tobacco.

When ambassador to Portugal (1559–1561), Nicot came upon this plant during a visit to the royal pharmacy in Lisbon, whence it had been brought by New World explorers. Finding it interesting, he sent samples to Catherine de Medicis, dowager queen of France, and her encouragement made smoking an instant success throughout Europe.

## Otaheite orange

A decorative pot plant of the citrus genus, bearing inedible fruits and named for the former name of Tahiti. The origin of the plant itself is unknown.

Otaheite has also given its name to an applelike fruit, an arrowroot, and a gooseberry. Only the Otaheite apple is actually of Polynesian origin.

## Paris daisy

A variety of chrysanthemum, also known as the marguerite (French for "daisy"), named for the capital city of France.

The Parisii, a Gallic tribe, held the village (then called Lutetia) at the time of Caesar's conquest, and eventually they gave the City of Light its modern name.

## Parma violet

A particularly strong and sweet-smelling variety of violet, named for the northern Italian city of Parma.

## peony

A fragrant garden flower, named for the mythological Greek physician Paion, who supposedly discovered its medical virtues. The ancients used peony root as a cure for jaundice, kidney disease, and epilepsy. Today it is the state flower of Indiana.

## Poinciana

A genus of flowering tropical trees, named for Monsieur de Poinci, seventeenth-century governor of the French Antilles.

## Poinsettia

A genus of tropical American herbs, whose showy red leaf bracts (not true flowers) make it a popular Christmas plant, named for Joel Robert Poinsett (1799–1851), first United States minister to Mexico.

Dr. Poinsett, much interested in Mexican and Central American life, was the first to introduce the wild plant to cultivation.

## Rafflesia

A genus of stemless, leafless parasitic plants of Malaya, named for the founder of Singapore, Sir Thomas Stamford Raffles (1781–1826).

One species has the largest flower in the world—spanning three feet, weighing twenty pounds, and emitting a foul odor, which attracts its pollinating agent, the carrion fly.

## rose of Jericho

Not a true rose but an Asiatic plant distantly related to the poppy and named for ancient Jericho, probably the oldest known city in the world. Jericho, once located in Jordan, is now in Israel.

Also called the resurrection plant, the rose of Jericho expands when wet and rolls up when dry.

## rose of Sharon

Also not a true rose but a tall flowering shrub, related to the hibiscus and misnamed for a plant mentioned in the Bible. The original rose of Sharon, named for the Plains of Sharon, an area of land lying along Israel's seacoast north of Tel-Aviv, is thought to have been a type of flowering perennial like the tulip.

## Saint-John's-wort

A yellow-flowered perennial weed, noxious to cattle, named for John the Baptist because it was gathered on Saint John's eve (May 14), to ward off evil spirits.

## Saintpaulia

A genus of East African herbs—the best known being the African violet—named for the colonial administrator of German East Africa (now Tanzania), Baron Walter von Saint Paul.

## Saint-Peter's-wort

The popular name for several different blooming herbs, named for the Apostle Peter, either because it blooms about the time of the saint's feast day (June 29) or because the leaves resemble keys. Keys are the symbol of Saint Peter in accordance with Jesus' words:

> And I will give unto thee the keys of the kingdom of heaven: and whatsoever thou shalt bind on earth shall be bound in heaven: and whatsoever thou shalt loose on earth shall be loosed in heaven. (Matthew 16:19)

## Sansevieria

A genus of tropical African and Asian herbs of the lily family, named for Raimondo di Sangro (1710–1771), prince of San Severo, Italy. The best known of Sansevieria is the snake plant.

## Shasta daisy

A large-flowered snow-white garden daisy, developed from the common oxeye daisy by the famed horticulturist Luther Burbank (1849–1926) and named for Mount Shasta in northern California.

Incidentally, Burbank, California ("beautiful downtown Burbank"), is *not* named for Luther Burbank, as one might think, but for David Burbank, a Los Angeles dentist, who subdivided the original tract.

## Shortia

A genus of perennial flowering evergreens named for Charles W. Short (1794–1863), American physician and botanist. Dr. Short explored the region west of the Alleghenies, collecting and classifying the flora.

## sisal

A West Indian agave whose plant yields a fiber, also called sisal, used in making rope and binder twine, named for the town of Sisal in northern Yucatan, Mexico.

## Spanish bayonet

A short-trunked yucca of tropical America with stiff, spine-tipped leaves that are shaped like sword blades. A smaller relative of the bayonet is called *Spanish dagger*.

## Star of Bethlehem

Any of several different plants of the lily family with star-shaped white flowers, named for the star that guided the wise men to Bethlehem at Christ's birth.

## Venus's-flytrap

An insectivorous plant of the sundew family, named for the Roman goddess of love. The leaf traps, when open, somewhat resemble seashells and may have reminded early botanists of Botticelli's "The Birth of Venus," which shows the goddess riding shoreward on a seashell.

Other plants named for the goddess are Venus's hair, a maidenhair fern, and Venus's-looking-glass, a plant with delicately star-shaped flowers.

## Virginia cowslip

Not a true cowslip but a blue-flowering herb of the borage family, native to the east coast of North America, which reminded Virginia colonists of their native English flower, named for Elizabeth I, the Virgin Queen.

## Weigela

A genus of flowering shrubs, widely cultivated for its showy deep-pink blossoms, named for Christian Ehrenfried von Weigel (1748–1831), German physician and botanist.

## Zinnia

A genus of tropical American herbs, now widely cultivated and developed as garden flowers, named for Johann Gottfried Zinn (1727–1759), German botanist and physician and friend of Linnaeus.

Dr. Zinn was the author of the first book on the anatomy of the eye, published in 1755, and his name has been given to several anatomical structures, mostly related to the eye: Zinn's circlet, Zinn's central artery, Zinn's corona, Zinn's ligament, Zinn's membrane, Zinn's tendon, Zinn's zonule. It may have been the bright eyelike look of the zinnia that prompted Linnaeus to choose Zinn's name for the plant.

# TREES . . .

## cedar of Lebanon

An evergreen tree, native to the Near East and named for the ancient land of Lebanon. Cedars of Lebanon produce a fragrant wood, grow unusually tall for the area, and attain a great age. They are employed in the Bible as symbols of strength and pride:

> The voice of the Lord breaketh the cedars; yea the Lord breaketh the cedars of Lebanon. (Psalms 29:5) . . . For the

day of the Lord of hosts shall be upon everyone that is proud
and lofty, and upon every one that is lifted up; and he shall
be brought low: And upon all the cedars of Lebanon, that
are high and lifted up. (Isaiah 2:12–13) . . .

King Solomon used the wood of this great tree to build the temple of
Jerusalem.

## Cinchona

A genus of trees native to the Andes and named for Doña Francisca
Henriquez de Ribera, countess of Cinchon (1576–1639). The countess
used the bark of this tree to cure herself of a fever and in gratitude
introduced it to Europe, where its use quickly spread. It is the source of
quinine.

## Douglas fir

Not a true fir but an evergreen in a class by itself, a timber tree named
for David Douglas (1798–1834), Scottish botanist. Sent to North
America in 1823, Douglas was the first to describe this magnificent
species, which often tops two hundred feet in height and more than
twelve feet in girth.

Douglas firs, growing in enormous stands all over the Pacific
Northwest, are America's second-tallest trees (after the sequoia) and
supply two thirds of all our lumber.

## Judas tree

A tree of a Eurasian genus, which produces showy red flowers in early
spring, named Judas because it is said in legend to be the tree on which
Judas Iscariot hanged himself.

## Kalmia

A genus of North American trees of the heath family, named for Per
Kalm, an eighteenth-century Swedish botanist. Included in the genus

are such charming species as the mountain laurel, sheep laurel, and pale laurel.

In 1748, Kalm, a student of the great Linnaeus, was sent to America by the Swedish government to bring back an account of the natural resources of the New World. His *Travels in North America* (1770–1771) is regarded as one of the most readable and reliable sources for colonial American history.

The Kalmias have quite an interesting history. The plant called sheepkill (sheep laurel) has decimated many flocks, because livestock die from eating its leaves. The Delaware Indians are thought to have used it to commit suicide. But no plant is more beloved than the mountain laurel, whose showy pink flowers have made it the state flower of Connecticut and Pennsylvania.

## Lombardy popular

A plume-shaped variety of black poplar, common throughout southern Europe and named for the northern Italian district of Lombardy, of which Milan is the capital. Northern Europeans, crossing the Alps, probably first came upon this attractive Mediterranean tree in Lombardy.

## Macadamia tree

A genus of evergreens native to Australia, named for Australian chemist John Macadam. One species of macadamia is widely cultivated for its nuts.

## Montezuma cypress

A Mexican cypress of great girth, named for the last Aztec emperor, Montezuma II (1466–1520). The native name for this tree, *ahuehuete,* means "old man of the water" in Nahuatl, for cypress trees often grow in bodies of water.

## Paulownia

A genus of trees of Chinese origin, named for Anna Paulovna, a Russian princess and queen of William II, King of the Netherlands

(1792–1849). Anna and William are great-grandparents of the present Dutch queen.


## Saint Thomas tree

A tropical shrub of Asia and Africa whose yellow flower has a prominent red blotch, named for the Apostle Thomas. According to legend, Thomas carried the Gospel to southern India and was martyred there, and people believed that at his death he bled on the flowers of the Saint Thomas tree, leaving the red spot.


## Sequoia (California redwood)

A genus of coniferous trees of enormous size and striking red wood, named for the Cherokee scholar Sequoya (1770–1840). Sequoya labored for twelve years to develop an alphabet that would adequately express the sounds of his native language—a literary feat never matched by any other individual. Armed with Sequoya's eighty-five-character syllabary, the Cherokee became literate in a matter of months.

Sequoias, native to eastern California, are believed to be the largest living things in the world and among the oldest. The "General Sherman," which may be thousands of years old, stands 272 feet tall and has a girth of 79 feet, but even that is dwarfed by the "Howard Libbey," which soars to 367 feet, the height of a thirty-story building.


# VINES . . .

## Bignonia

A genus of American and Japanese flowering vines, closely related to the trumpet creeper, named for the librarian to King Louis XV, Abbé Jean-Paul Bignon.


## Bougainvillea

A genus of tropical American flowering vines of the four-o'clock family, widely cultivated in warm climates as a garden ornamental, named for French explorer Louis Antoine de Bougainville (1729–1811).

Bougainville, the first Frenchman to circumnavigate the globe, excelled in several fields. As a naval officer, he served under Montcalm in the French and Indian War and under De Grasse in the American Revolution. His two-volume work on integral calculus earned him an appointment to the Royal Society (British), and he was later made a member of the Institut de France. In 1766–69, he led a French expedition of exploration across the Pacific, which touched at Samoa, Tahiti, the New Hebrides, the Solomons, and New Guinea. Later he was made a senator and a count of the empire by Napoleon.

In addition to the handsome vine that bears his name, two straits and the largest of the Solomon Islands have been named for Bougainville.

## Wisteria

A genus of Asiatic and North American vines with pendulous blossoms, widely grown as an ornamental climber, named in honor of Caspar Wistar (1761–1818), pioneer American anatomist.

Dr. Wistar, grandson of one of America's earliest glassmakers, wrote the first American textbook on anatomy.

# GRASS . . .

Grass is by far humankind's most important plant. It constitutes one quarter of the earth's vegetation, having more than 7,000 species. These include sugarcane, bamboo, rice, millet, sorghum, corn, wheat, barley, oats, and rye.

## Bermuda grass

A trailing grass that proliferates itself by means of runners, which is native to southern Europe but named for the Bermuda Islands because of its widespread use as a lawn grass in warm climates.

Bermuda itself, a group of 120 limestone islands and inlets, was named for Juan Bermúdez, a Spanish sea captain who sailed there in 1515.

## Job's tears

An Asiatic grass which produces hard white seeds reminiscent of the tears shed by the biblical Job when he was made to suffer afflictions in a test of his loyalty to God. The seeds, also called Job's tears, are frequently strung into necklaces or rosaries.

## Johnson grass

A tall sorghum grass, which spreads by means of underground rhizomes, named for American agriculturist William Johnson. Johnson grass was first imported into the United States from Turkey in 1835 as a forage hay, but it escaped into cropland, where it is a serious pest to cotton and other crops and very difficult to eradicate.

## Kentucky bluegrass

A fine pasture and lawn grass, native to both Europe and America and named for Kentucky, where it reaches its best growth and is widely used as pasturage for thoroughbred horses. The term "bluegrass" originally applied to a different species of grass which had a bluish-green stem, but later it came to be used of this variety, which is purely green.

## timothy

An important forage grass, native to Europe, named for Timothy Hanson, an eighteenth-century American farmer. Hanson, a New Yorker, is said to have been the first to introduce timothy to the South, about 1720.

It is sometimes also called herd's grass (for John Herd, an early enthusiast), June grass, and cattail.

## Zoysia grass

A genus of Asiatic grasses widely used as a lawn grass, named for Karl von Zois, a German botanist. Zoysias, which form a dense and springy turf, are popular as golf-course grass.

# PLANT DISEASES . . .

## Dutch elm disease

A fungus disease of elm trees carried by bark beetles and unfairly blamed on the Dutch because it was first studied and described by pathologists in the Netherlands. The disease was first imported into the United States in lumber shipped from France around 1930 and since then has spread rapidly throughout the eastern and midwestern states.

## Jonathan freckle

A storage disease of apples that produces a "freckle" or discoloration of the skin and is named for the Jonathan apple, which is especially susceptible to it. Jonathans, in turn, were named for Jonathan Hasbrouck, a resident of the Hudson Valley, where it was first developed, who helped to publicize it.

# · 3 ·

# The Mineral
# Kingdom

The Earth's crust has given humankind natural resources that have enabled us to live better lives. Minerals of all kinds have been extracted, processed, and utilized—gems for our fingers, radioactive elements for our nuclear plants, metals for our tools, and stones for our buildings.

## almandite

A deep-red variety of garnet named for the ancient town of Alabanda in Caria (now western Turkey), where gems were cut and sold.

## bauxite

An ore which is the chief source of commercial aluminum, named for Les Baux, near Arles in Provence, France, where the mineral was first found in 1821.

## bentonite

An aluminum silicate clay named for Fort Benton, Montana, where it was first discovered. The fort, in turn, was named for the politician Thomas Hart Benton (1782–1858).

## berkelium

A man-made radioactive element named for the city of Berkeley, California, where it was discovered in December 1949. A renowned team of scientists—S. G. Thompson, A. Ghiorso, and G. T. Seaborg—working at the Lawrence Radiation Laboratory, U.C. Berkeley, isolated the element by bombarding another element, americium, with helium ions.

The same team also discovered *californium* two months later.

## boson

A particle, such as a photon or meson, having zero or integral spin, named for Satyendranath Bose (b. 1894), a brilliant Indian mathematician. Bose collaborated with Albert Einstein to formulate the Bose-Einstein statistics.

## bronze

An alloy of copper and tin, the oldest of man-made metals, named for Brundisium (now Brindisi) in southern Italy, a city famed for its exports of bronze.

## brookite

A form of titanium dioxide, named for English mineralogist Henry J. Brooke (1771–1857).

## cairngorm

A yellow or brown form of crystalline quartz, named for the Cairngorm Mountains, a range of the Grampians in north-central Scotland. The cairngorm is a favorite jewel among Scots and usually forms the large stone in the brooch that fastens the Highland plaid.

## calaverite

A yellowish ore containing both gold and silver elements, named for Calaveras County, California, where it was discovered. The Spaniards found human skulls—*calaveras*—in this area in 1830.

## carnotite

A uranium and vanadium ore, first described in 1899 and named for Marie Adolphe Carnot (1839–1920), a chemist and France's inspector general of mines.

A ton of carnotite yields ten pounds of uranium oxide, fifty-five pounds of vanadium, and 1/1000 of a gram of radium.

## chalcedony

A variety of quartz named for the ancient Greek city of Chalcedon on the Bosporus (now Kadikoy, Turkey).

Since ancient times, chalcedony has been the favorite of gem carvers. Found in various color phases, chalcedony is also known as onyx, agate, bloodstone, chrysoprase, sardonyx, carnelian, and cat's eye.

## colemanite

Hydrated calcium borate, main source of borax, named for William T. Coleman (1824–1893), owner of the mine in Death Valley, California, where it was found in 1882. Coleman was one of the pioneers of the borax industry and its famous twenty-mule teams.

## copper

A common metallic element, known since before recorded time and named for the Mediterranean island of Cyprus, which produced the best copper. Our word "copper" is a corrupt form of Cyprus.

Excellent grades of copper were mined on Cyprus as early as 2500 B.C., whence huge supplies were shipped to Egypt and other parts of the ancient world. The ore, man's first important metal, was used for weapons, tools, and household utensils.

## cordierite

A silicate of iron, magnesium, and aluminum, named for French geologist Pierre Louis Cordier (1777–1861) who first described it.

## covellite

A mineral containing 66.4 percent copper, named for Italian chemist Nicholas Covelli (1790–1829), who discovered it.

## dolomite

A calcium and magnesium carbonate, named in honor of Déodat de Dolomieu (1750–1801), French geologist who was the first to describe it, in 1791.

Dolomitic limestones occur in vast masses in some areas, notably the Tyrolean Alps, where a particular range is called The Dolomites for the chief form of rock of which it is composed.

## dumortierite

A borosilicate mineral named for Eugène Dumortier, nineteenth-century French paleontologist. It is much used in the manufacture of such products as porcelain and spark plugs.

## franklinite

A magnetic mineral containing oxide of iron and zinc, named for Franklin Furnace (now Franklin), New Jersey, where it was mined and smelted.

## gadolinium

A vitreous silicate of iron and other elements, discovered in 1886 and named in honor of Johann Gadolin (1760–1852), a Finnish chemist. It is the fortieth most abundant element in the world and an important source of rare earths.

## gallium

A metallic element usually obtained as a byproduct of aluminum, named for its discoverer, French chemist Paul *Lecoq* de Boisbaudran

(1838–1912). Lecoq ("the cock") translated his name from French into Latin, *gallus*.

## garnierite

A greenish hydrated silicate of nickel and magnesium, named for French geologist Jules Garnier (1839–1904).

## goethite

An iron ore named for the renowned German poet, Johann Wolfgang von Goethe (1749–1832). Among the poet's many scientific interests was the science of mineralogy, which he studied in connection with his official position as an adviser to the duke of Weimar.

## greenockite

A cadmium sulfide named for its discoverer, Charles Murray Cathcart, Lord Greenock (1783–1859). Cadmium, derived from greenockite, is chiefly used to plate steel and other alloys as a protection against corrosion.

Lord Greenock was quartermaster general under Wellington at Waterloo and later served as commander-in-chief in Canada.

## hafnium

A metallic element discovered in Copenhagen in 1922 and named for the Latin form of the city's name, Hafnia. Its discoverers were George de Hevesy, a Hungarian chemist, and Dirk Coster, a Dutch physicist.

Because of its high melting point, hafnium is used for nuclear-reactor control rods.

## heulandite

A form of hydrous silicate, composed of calcium, sodium, and aluminum and named for a British collector of minerals, Henry Heuland.

## hiddenite

A yellow or green spoduneme used as a gemstone and named for its discoverer, American mineralogist William E. Hidden (1853–1918).

## holmium

A rare-earth metallic element, discovered by Swedish chemist T. Cleve in 1879 and named for the Latin form of Stockholm, his home city.

## iridium

A metallic element whose salts are often brightly colored, named by the man who isolated it in 1802, British chemist Smithson Tennant, for Iris, the Greek goddess of the rainbow.

Iridium, which is highly resistant to all acids and salts, is often used to harden platinum and precision instruments, and to form alloys which can resist high temperatures.

## itacolumite

A micaceous quartzite or form of sandstone, named for a mountain in the state of Minas Gerais, Brazil, where it is found in abundance. Itacolumite is unusual in that, if sliced as thin as one half inch, it will bend under its own weight without breaking.

## kernite

A hydrous sodium borate, an important source of borax, named for Kern County, California, where a large deposit was discovered.

Kern County itself took its name from Edward M. Kern, a topographer and artist with Fremont's expeditions of exploration.

## kunzite

A semiprecious gemstone of pinkish color, named in honor of George Frederick Kunz (1856–1932), an American authority on gems and ancient jewelry. Kunz was vice-president of Tiffany and Company from 1907 to 1932.

## lawrencium

A laboratory-produced radioactive element, discovered in 1961 by a group of internationally known scientists and named in honor of the American physicist Ernest Orlando Lawrence (1901–1959). In 1939, Lawrence won the Nobel prize for his invention of the cyclotron, and during World War II, he helped develop the atomic bomb.

## magnesia

A manganese oxide named for Magnesia, a metal-rich region near Thessaly in ancient Greece. Magnesia has many uses but its best known is as an aid for stomach acidity and as a laxative.

The metal-attracting iron ore called *magnet*—"Stone of Magnesia"—got its name from the same area in Greece.

## mendelevium

A radioactive element produced by a group of U.C. Berkeley scientists in 1955, named for Dmitri Ivanovich Mendeleev (1834–1907), famed Russian chemist. Mendeleev developed the classification table of chemical elements.

## mercury

A heavy silver-white poisonous metal, the only metal that has a liquid form at ordinary room temperatures, named for Mercury, fleet-footed messenger of the Roman gods.

Also known as quicksilver, mercury has many uses. Because it will not wet glass and has high density and low vapor pressure, it is employed in thermometers, barometers, and vacuum gauges. It has excellent conductivity and hence is used to make electrical switches and relays. It is found in heat engines, rectifiers for alternating current, ultraviolet lamps, and a hundred industrial devices.

## millerite

A nickel sulfide named for the British mineralogist who developed a system of crystallography, William H. Miller (1801–1880).

## Monel metal

Trademark name (owned by the International Nickel Company) for an alloy of nickel and copper with other metals, named for INC president Ambrose Monel (1873–1921).

## monzonite

An igneous rock, containing several minerals plus large amounts of orthoclase and plagioclase feldspar, named for Mount Monzoni in the Italian Alps, where its largest known deposit is located. Feldspar is the most abundant mineral on earth.

## morganite

A gemstone of pink beryl, named for American financier John Pierpont Morgan (1837–1913).

## niobium

A ductile metallic element, extracted from tantalite and, because of its source, named for the mythological Niobe.

Niobe, daughter of Tantalus (see *tantalium*), had six sons and six daughters, and on this account boasted that she was a greater mother than the goddess Leto, who had only one son and one daughter. For Niobe's arrogance, Leto's children, Apollo and Artemis, slew Niobe's twelve, and in grief she was changed to a stone, out of which flowed a spring, representing her tears.

Niobium was discovered in 1801 by a British chemist, Charles Hatchett (1765–1847), who named it columbium. But in 1844 it was renamed niobium by German chemist Heinrich Rose, and this name was confirmed by international agreement in 1949. American metallurgists still sometimes call it columbium.

## palladium

A silver-white metallic element, often found mixed with platinum and named for the asteroid Pallas, discovered in the same year. Pallas, in turn, was named for the Greek goddess of wisdom, called Pallas Athena and often associated with Athens.

## plutonium

A radioactive element, first produced by Glenn Seaborg and other scientists at U.C. Berkeley in 1940 and named for the planet Pluto. This was in accordance with the practice at the time of naming such elements by the order of the planets (see *uranium*).

Plutonium, one of the most famous (or infamous) radioactive elements, was obtained by using a cyclotron to bombard uranium 235 with neutrons. Plutonium-239 was a major ingredient in the atomic bomb dropped on Nagasaki August 9, 1945, which killed or injured 75,000 people.

## polonium

A radioactive metallic element, occurring in pitchblende and other uranium ores, discovered by Marie and Pierre Curie and named by Madame Curie for her homeland, Poland.

## promethium

A metallic element of the rare-earth group, isolated and identified in April 1946 and named for the mythological Prometheus. To the scientists who discovered the element, the nuclear furnace they used was reminiscent of the fire stolen by Prometheus from heaven to give to man.

## samarskite

A rare velvet-black mineral with a glassy or resinous luster, containing a large number of rare-earth elements, named for Russian mining official V. Y. von Samarsky, who discovered it in the Ural Mountains.

## sard

A variety of carnelian (itself a variety of chalcedony) named for Sardis, capital of ancient Lydia (now Sart, Turkey). Sard and carnelian both were much used in early civilizations for the carving of seals by the intaglio method.

## scandium

A lightweight metallic element, most commonly found in Scandinavia and named by its discoverer, Lars Nilson, after Scandia, the Latin name for what is now Sweden and parts of Denmark.

## smithsonite

A white zinc carbonate, which effervesces on contact with acid, named for English chemist and mineralogist James Smithson (1765–1829).

Smithson is best known as the founder of the Smithsonian Institution in Washington, D.C. The illegitimate son of the first duke of Northumberland, the bachelor Smithson bequeathed £100,000 to the United States government to set up an "establishment for the increase and diffusion of knowledge among men." No one knows the reason for this bequest, since Smithson had never set foot on American soil and had never been known to express special interest in the United States, but it ultimately resulted in one of the world's great educational and cultural institutions.

## sperrylite

A platinum arsenide, named for nineteenth-century Canadian mineralogist F. L. Sperry. Sperrylite is the only platinum compound known to occur in nature.

## spessartite

A form of garnet containing manganese and named for the Spessart mountain range in West Germany, a wine and fruit-growing region north of the Main River.

## taconite

A low-grade iron ore found principally in the Taconic Range of Vermont's Green Mountains. The Taconics cross the Massachusetts–New York border between Williamstown and Stephentown.

## tantalum

An extremely durable metallic element, named for the mythological king of Sipylus, Tantalus. For an insult to the gods, Tantalus was condemned to suffer unappeased hunger and thirst (see *tantalize*) without dying.

This indestructibility is what caused Anders G. Ekeberg, a Swedish chemist, to name his discovery (1802) after Tantalus, for tantalum has a high melting point and is resistant to most chemicals, which makes it an ideal substance for surgical instruments and parts for nuclear-reactor plants.

## tanzanite

A deep-blue variety of gemstone, discovered in 1968 and named for its country of origin, Tanzania.

## thenardite

A form of sodium sulfate found in salt lakes and named for Louis Jacques Thénard (1777–1857), a French chemist and an inspired teacher. Thénard is credited with the discovery of hydrogen peroxide and co-discovery of boron, and his four-volume textbook on chemistry was considered the standard European textbook for a quarter of a century. (See *Thénard's blue.*)

## titanium

A strong, lustrous gray metallic element, corrosion-resistant, named for the Titans, mighty earth giants of ancient Greek mythology.

Titanium was discovered in 1790 by William Gregor, a British clergyman, and named by German chemist Martin Heinrich Klaproth (1743–1817). Klaproth had previously named uranium after the planet Uranus, which made selection of "titanium" fairly easy, since Uranus was the father of the six Titans.

## torbernite

A phosphate of uranium and copper named for Swedish chemist and physicist Torbern Olaf Bergman (1735–1784). Bergman was the first to obtain nickel in a pure state and is known for his studies of the rainbow and the aurora borealis.

## travertine

A mineral containing massive layers of calcium carbonate, formed from deposits by springs (especially hot springs) and named for the French form of Tiburtinus, "of Tibur." Tibur was an old town on the Anio (now Aniene) River, now called Tivoli.

Stalactites and stalagmites found in caverns are usually formed of travertine, as is a form of the mineral known as Mexican onyx or alabaster.

## tremolite

A silicate mineral, named for the Swiss valley Tremola, where it was first found.

## troostite

A type of red crystalline willemite (a form of zinc silicate) named for the American geologist Gerald Troost (1776–1850).

In 1807 Troost was hired by the king of the Netherlands to journey throughout Europe collecting minerals for him.

## turquoise

A gemstone, consisting chiefly of copper-aluminum phosphate, found in Arizona, New Mexico, and Persia but named for Turkey, because the first samples of it reached Europe by way of the Ottoman Empire.

The startling blue-green color of the *"pierre turquoise"* (French: "Turkish stone") gave it special value to the people who loved and used it: Egyptians, Persians, Aztecs, Incas, and American Indians.

## uranium

A radioactive metallic element, discovered in the same decade as the planet Uranus and named for it. Uranium was discovered in 1789 by Martin Heinrich Klaproth (1743–1817), a German chemist, while he was experimenting with pitchblende.

Its uses have varied considerably. Antoine Henri Becquerel and Marie Curie discovered its radioactive properties at the turn of the century, and Otto Kahn used it to generate nuclear energy at the outset of World War II.

## uvarovite

An emerald-green garnet, named for Count Sergei S. Uvarov (1785–1855), Russian statesman and author.

## vanadium

A malleable metallic element, highly corrosion-resistant, used in the production of high-strength structural steel, and named for Vanadis (Freya), the Norse goddess of beauty and fertility, because of the beautiful colors of its compounds.

## vesuvianite

A silicate of calcium, magnesium, iron, and aluminum, named for Mount Vesuvius near Naples, because of its occurrence in the lava ejected by this volcano.

## willemite

A form of zinc silicate, named for Willem I, king of the Netherlands.

## witherite

A mineral, rich in barium, named for William Withering (1741–1799), English doctor, who first analyzed it. Glasslike witherite is used for such unrelated products as medicines and rat poisons.

## wollastonite

A calcium metasilicate mineral named for British chemist William Hyde Wollaston (1766–1828).

## zoisite

A calcium aluminum silicate, often used in fancy stonework, named in honor of its discoverer, Baron Sigismund Zois von Edelstein, a Slovenian nobleman (1747–1819).

# Part 2

---

# HOMO SAPIENS: MAN AND WOMAN

# · 4 ·

# The Mind:
# It Takes All Kinds

Being able to stand erect and having a workable thumb are the chief attributes that separate the caveman and the corporate executive from the tail-wagging dog. People are fascinating social animals. The many ways that we think and react toward each other make our world an exciting place.

## Amazon

A strong, aggressive, perhaps masculine type of woman. In Greek mythology, the Amazons ("Breastless") were a tribe of female warriors located in what is now southern Russia. It is said they cut off or burned off the right breast in order to facilitate their use of the bow. Hippolyte, their queen, was slain by Hercules.

## argus

A person who is very vigilant, alert, or watchful, named for the mythical Greek Argus, an earthborn giant with eyes all over his body, only half of which were closed in sleep at any one time.

Argus was ordered by Hera to watch over Io, Zeus's beloved, whom he had changed into the shape of a heifer, but Hermas lulled him to sleep and then cut off his head. Hera then transferred his eyes to the peacock's tail.

## atlas (the man)

Anyone who sustains a heavy burden, named for the mighty Titan

Atlas, who carried the heavens on his shoulders. It also denotes a book of maps (see *atlas, the book*).

## Babbitt

A crude and vulgar worshiper of material success at the expense of artistic values, named for the fictional character George F. Babbitt, in Sinclair Lewis' 1922 novel of the same name.

## benedict

A newly married man, especially one who had expected to remain a bachelor, named for the fictional character Benedick in Shakespeare's *Much Ado About Nothing*.

## Bluebeard

A man who marries and kills a number of women, named for the fictional character Bluebeard in the fairy tale by Charles Perrault (1628–1703).

Perrault was also the author of such familiar stories as "Sleeping Beauty," "Red Riding Hood," "Puss in Boots," and "Cinderella."

## Bohemian

An unconventional, usually artistic person, named for Bohemia (now Czechoslovakia), which was for many centuries a land of ethnic and religious upheaval.

Bohemia takes its name from the Boii, a Celtic people who lived partly in northern Italy and partly in central Germany, and at one time it was thought that the Gypsies ("Bohemians" par excellence) came from there.

## Boswell

Someone who admires another and meticulously records his words and actions, named for James Boswell (1740–1795), who thus recorded the doings of Dr. Samuel Johnson, English lexicographer and essayist.

Boswell, a Scot by birth, met Johnson on a trip to London in 1763, took careful note of the great man's conversation, and wrote a highly regarded biography *The Life of Samuel Johnson, LL.D*, which was published the year after Johnson's death.

## bugger

A sodomite or a contemptible person, named for a corrupted form of "Bulgar." The Bulgarians, who adhered to the Eastern Orthodox Church, were regarded by Western Europeans as heretics and hence people of little worth.

## caesar

Emperor or powerful ruler, sometimes a dictator, named for Gaius Julius Caesar (100–44 B.C.), and his successors—the Caesars.

A brilliant general and politician, Caesar made himself ruler of Rome in 46 B.C. and was assassinated two years later. His grandnephew Octavian then became the first emperor under the name of Augustus.

Both the German *Kaiser* and the Russian *czar* are forms of "caesar."

## Casanova

A man who courts women indiscriminately and with few moral restrictions, named for Giovanni Jacopo Casanova (1725–1798), Italian adventurer. Casanova wrote a twelve-volume set of memoirs, which are valued chiefly as a picture of eighteenth-century European life.

## cassandra

A person who prophesies misfortune or habitually looks on the dark side, named for the daughter of King Priam of Troy. Cassandra, given the gift of prophecy by Apollo, nevertheless spurned the god's advances and was punished by never being believed, although she correctly foretold the fall of Troy.

## catamite

A boy kept by a man for the purpose of sexual perversion, named for Catamitus (Latin form for the Greek Ganymede), cupbearer to the gods.

## charlatan

A fraud, especially a medical quack, named for the French form of *cerretano* (Italian: native of Cerreto), an Italian village near Spoleto famous for its quacks.

## Charlie McCarthy

A yes-man or person controlled by another, named for ventriloquist Edgar Bergen's famous wiseacre dummy.

## chauvinist

Anyone who spouts excessive or blind patriotism, named for Nicolas Chauvin, a French soldier, pugnaciously loyal to Napoleon.

Chauvin, severely wounded in battle, was rewarded with a sword, a red ribbon, and a small pension, but was immortalized in several French plays, notably Cogniard's *The Tricolor Cockade*.

## Chesterfieldian

An adjective describing an elegant and slightly cynical man, named for Philip Dormer Stanhope, fourth earl of Chesterfield (1694–1773), whose letters to his illegitimate son taught manners without morals.

## Cinderella

Someone lifted suddenly from obscurity to fame and fortune, named for the heroine of Charles Perrault's famous fairy tale.

## Colonel Blimp

A pompous reactionary, named for David Low's cartoon character in the London *Evening Standard* and *Star* during the 1930's and 1940's.

## Corinthian

A fast-living, playboy sort of person, named for the ancient Greek city of Corinth, which was famous in its day for wealth and wickedness.

## cupid

Anyone who plays the role of matchmaker, named for Cupid, the son of Venus, the Roman goddess of love, usually depicted as a plump cherub carrying a bow and arrows. It was thought that a man or woman who fell deeply in love must have been pierced by one of Cupid's arrows.

## Damon and Pythias

Extremely close, nearly inseparable friends, named for two fourth-century-B.C. Roman citizens of Syracuse.

When Pythias was condemned to death for plotting against the ruler of his city, Damon took his place in prison while his friend concluded some business elsewhere. To the astonishment of everyone except Damon, Pythias returned in time for his execution and released his friend, which so moved the ruler that he pardoned them both.

## Darby and Joan

A quiet, plain, very close elderly couple, named for the fictional pair in John Woodfall's ballad "The Happy Old Couple."

## Diogenes

A seeker of truth or of honest people, named for a fourth-century-B.C. Greek philosopher. Diogenes is said to have hunted through the streets of Athens in broad daylight, carrying a lantern, looking for "an honest man."

When visited by Alexander the Great, who asked if he could do something for such a learned man, Diogenes replied, "Yes, you can step aside and not get between me and the sun."

## Don Juan

A woman-chaser or libertine, named for the fictional character of many literary treatments. A young nobleman of Seville, Don Juan indiscriminately and unscrupulously pursued women and was punished when the statue of the father of one of his victims came to life.

*Don Juanism* is a psychological term for male sexual promiscuity, usually based on feelings of inadequacy.

## doubting Thomas

A habitual skeptic, named for the Apostle Thomas who refused to believe his colleagues' word that Jesus had risen from the dead:

> Except I shall see in his hands the print of the nails, and put my finger into the print of the nails, and thrust my hand into his side, I will not believe. (John 20:25)

## Draconian

Harsh or rigorous, said particularly of laws or rules, named for Draco, a seventh-century-B.C. Athenian lawgiver. Draco decreed the death penalty for nearly every offense, however minor.

## Dracula

One who lives by drawing strength, usually psychological, from another person, named for Bram Stoker's fictional count, a centuries-old vampire.

# Dryasdust

A dull, bookish, pedantic person, named for Dr. Jonas Dryasdust, a literary creation of Sir Walter Scott.

# dunce

A stupid or slow-witted person, named for John Duns Scotus (1266–1308), Scottish scholastic theologian.

Although he himself was regarded as a brilliant orator and philosopher, named Doctor Subtilis ("learned discriminator"), his followers eventually won a reputation for obstructionist and caviling practices that gave the term "dunce" its pejorative meaning.

# Electra complex

A Freudian term for a girl's sexual attraction to her father, named for the mythological daughter of Agamemnon, who urged her brother Orestes to murder their mother, Clytemnestra, in revenge for Clytemnestra's murder of their father.

# erotic

Arousing sexual feelings, named for the Greek god of love, Eros, son of Aphrodite (counterpart of the Roman Cupid). Freud used the term "eros" to signify the positive life force that underlies our sexual instincts.

# Fagin

A man who corrupts the young, specifically one who teaches children to steal, named for the fictional character in Charles Dickens' *Oliver Twist*.

# Falstaffian

Fat, jovial, coarse, and licentious, named for Sir John Falstaff, the engaging rogue in Shakespeare's plays *Henry IV* and *The Merry Wives of Windsor*.

## Frankenstein monster

Something that grows beyond the control of its creator and eventually must be destroyed, named for the fictional monster in Mary Shelley's novel *Frankenstein*.

In the story Baron Victor von Frankenstein creates a manlike being out of parts of corpses, and it ultimately destroys him and itself. Many people mistakenly use the term "Frankenstein" to refer to the monster itself, although this is technically inaccurate.

## Freudian slip

An unintentional slip of the tongue which, according to Dr. Sigmund Freud (1856–1939), reveals repressed thoughts and feelings.

## Galahad

A pure and altruistic man, devoted to some selfless cause, named for Sir Galahad of the Arthurian legend. Galahad, the illegitimate son of Lancelot and Elaine, was the only member of the Round Table qualified to sit in the Siege Perilous and ultimately to find the Holy Grail.

## gascon

A braggart, an amusing swaggerer, named for the district in southwestern France, whose people had a reputation as boasters.

This characteristic has been portrayed in many works of fiction, notably Alexandre Dumas' *The Three Musketeers* (whose hero D'Artagnan is a Gascon), Rostand's *Cyrano de Bergerac*, and Dante's *Paradiso*.

The term "gasconade" means a long-winded, blustering boast of one's own prowess.

## goon

A stupid, lumpish thug, named in part for Elzie Segar's cartoon character Alice the Goon in *Thimble Theatre* ("Popeye").

In the labor movement, a goon is a strong-arm enforcer hired by management, and the term has also been used as a nasty pejorative for a black man, a German (during World War II), and an unattractive member of the opposite sex.

## Gorgon

A repulsive-looking woman, named for the mythological Gorgons of ancient Greece—three sisters, Stheno, Euryale, and Medusa—who had snakes for hair, brass hands, and scales all over their bodies and could turn anyone who glanced at them to stone.

## Greek chorus

A group of people expressing mindlessly similar views on one particular topic, named for the band of dancers and singers who commented on the dramatic events in a classical Greek play.

## Hamlet

An equivocator, unable to make up his mind, named for the principal character in Shakespeare's play of the same name. The fictional Prince of Denmark could not decide whether or not to take his stepfather's life in revenge for the murder of his father.

## harlequin

A buffoon or clown, named for the stock character Harlequin in the Italian Commedia dell' Arte. Harlequin wears spangled, particolored clothes, and consequently anything mottled or colored in variegated fashion can be said to be "harlequined."

## harpy

An unbearably nagging, parasitic woman, named for the Harpies in Greek mythology, monsters with the heads of women and the trunks, tails, wings, and claws of vultures. Considered spirits of mischief, they tormented men and carried out the revenge of the gods against them.

## hector

A bragging bully, named for the Trojan warrior-prince in Homer's *Iliad*.

Hector, a brave and high-minded prince, does not deserve to have his name turned into a term of derogation. Nevertheless, when someone badgers, blusters, and domineers over another, we say that he is "hectoring."

## hermaphrodite

Something that has contradictory elements, specifically (in living things) both male and female sex organs, named for the mythological Hermaphroditus, son of Hermes and Aphrodite.

The nymph Salmacis loved the youth but was rejected by him, and in revenge she prayed that they be joined together in one body, and her prayer was answered.

In the animal kingdom, hermaphrodite forms are usually found in such invertebrates as worms, snails, slugs, and barnacles. (See also *hermaphrodite brig*.)

## highbinder

A corrupt politician, a professional swindler, or a hired hatchetman, named for a gang of vagrants, the Highbinders, in early New York City.

## hooker

A prostitute, named for Civil War general "Fighting Joe" Hooker, who arranged such distractions to bolster the morale of his men.

## Horatio Alger

An adjective describing a rapid rise from poverty to wealth, named for Horatio Alger (1832–1899), who wrote 135 novels for boys on the rags-to-riches theme.

Alger got his information about his famous "ragged Dicks" and "tattered Toms" firsthand from his experiences in the Newsboys Lodging House, a place he established in New York City for homeless youngsters.

## hypnosis

A sleeplike trance state into which a subject is put by an outside operator, named for Hypnos, the Greek god of sleep.

Hypnos was the twin brother of Thanatos, the god of death, and was sometimes considered the father of Morpheus, god of dreams.

## Jack the Ripper

A cold-blooded multimurderer of women, named for a self-named throat slitter who stalked the streets of London from August to November, 1888.

The original Jack the Ripper, who murdered five or more London prostitutes before his spree was over, was never officially found. Recently revealed evidence, however, indicates that he may possibly have been a member of the royal family—Edward, Duke of Clarence, a grandson of Queen Victoria and heir to the throne after his father, the Prince of Wales. Edward died in 1892.

Edward is believed to have harbored a hatred for prostitutes, which was implanted in him by his tutor, James Steven, whose homosexual leanings caused him to despise streetwalkers. But all this, of course, is unprovable theory only.

## jackanapes

An impudent and conceited coxcomb, named for Jac Napes, the nickname of William de la Pole, first duke of Suffolk (1396–1450). Suffolk displayed an ape's ball and chain on his coat of arms.

The duke led an interesting—if tragic—life. Taken prisoner by Joan of Arc at Jargeau in 1429, he was released two years later. As leader of the peace party at home, he was accused of selling out to French interests, and though at first he was sentenced to banishment, the ship on which he was sailing was stopped at sea, and the duke was beheaded.

## Janus-faced

Two-faced, deceitful, named for Janus, the Roman god of gates and doorways, who is depicted as having two faces, one looking forward into the future, the other looking back into the past.

January, the first month of the Roman year, was named for Janus, and we also get our word "janitor" from his name (a janitor was originally a doorman). The gates of Janus' principal temple were kept open in time of war. In the seven hundred years before the beginning of the Christian era, they were closed only four times.

## Jekyll-and-Hyde

An adjective describing someone whose character has two contrasting aspects or who leads a double life, named for the leading character in Robert Louis Stevenson's story "The Strange Case of Dr. Jekyll and Mr. Hyde."

Stevenson is thought to have been inspired by the real-life Deacon William Brodie (1741–1788), by day a respectable Edinburgh cabinetmaker and pillar of the church, but by night a burglar.

## jezebel

A wicked, shameless woman, named for the ninth-century-B.C. Phoenician princess who was famed for her cruelty. Married to Ahab, King of Israel, Jezebel wielded great power and had anyone who opposed her slain, including the prophets of the Lord.

## jovial

Good-humored and jolly, named for the Roman god Jupiter, who is also called Jove.

## laconic

Terse, brief in speech and manner, named for the Greek province of Laconia, home of the Spartans, who were famed for the shortness of their answers.

## Laocoon

An adjective used of anyone struggling with overwhelming forces, named for the mythical Trojan priest who tried to warn his people not to accept the Greeks' wooden horse and in punishment was crushed and strangled by two enormous sea serpents.

## laodicean

Indifferent and lukewarm about some idea, named for the city of Laodicea (near modern Denizli, Turkey), whose citizens are described thus in Revelations:

> I know thy works, that thou art neither cold nor hot: I would thou wert cold or hot. So then because thou art lukewarm, and neither cold nor hot, I will spue thee out of my mouth. (Revelation 3:15–16)

## lesbian

A homosexual female, named for the island of Lesbos in ancient Greece, home of the lyric poetess Sappho (610–580 B.C.) and her reputedly homosexual group.

## Lincolnesque

Said of anyone tall, gaunt, and grave, named for Abraham Lincoln, sixteenth President of the United States (1809–1865). Lincoln's appearance, though anything but handsome, was striking and memorable.

## Lothario

An indiscriminate seducer of women, named for the character Lothario in Nicholas Rowe's 1703 drama *The Fair Penitent*.

## lotus-eater

A person who gives himself up to daydreaming and pleasure, named for the Lotus-eaters in Homer's Odyssey, who lived a drugged and dreamy existence by feeding on the fruit of the lotus plant.

## Lucrezia Borgia

A female poisoner, named for the Italian noblewoman (1480–1519) who was believed (probably unjustly) to have poisoned her second husband and a brother.

The illegitimate daughter of Pope Alexander VI and sister of the infamous Cesare, Lucrezia was used as a political pawn by her family, who engaged and/or married her off to two Spanish noblemen and three Italian princes. In her later years, as duchess of Ferrara, she set up a brilliant court of poets and artists, and devoted her life to charity and education.

## Machiavellian

An adjective used to describe the actions of an unscrupulous and devious politician, named for Florentine philosopher Niccolò Machiavelli (1469–1527), whose book *The Prince* teaches that a ruler must use any means whatever in order to acquire and keep power.

## mafficking

An overjoyous reaction to some piece of good news, named for Mafeking Night, May 17, 1900. When the news reached London that the South African town of Mafeking, besieged by a Boer army for seven long months, had been relieved, it set off an orgy of rejoicing.

## magdalen

A reformed and penitent prostitute, named for the biblical Mary Magdalene.

Actually Mary Magdalene was not a prostitute at all but someone Jesus cured of possession (Luke 8:2), but her story immediately follows that of a sinning woman who threw herself at Jesus' feet (Luke 7:37 ff.), and this resulted in a mistaken connection between the two.

## man Friday

A right-hand man, a close and trusted employe who performs many difficult, often confidential tasks, named for the fictional Indian servant in Daniel Defoe's *Robinson Crusoe*.

Actually it is probably used more often today as "gal Friday," denoting a general office assistant.

## marplot

A stupid interferer, one who ruins the carefully laid plans of someone else, named for the character Marplot in Susanna Centlivre's 1709 drama *The Busy Body*.

## martinet

A harsh and rigid military disciplinarian, named for Jean Martinet, seventeenth-century French army officer, who devised a new system of drill. Colonel Martinet is credited, along with the engineer Vauban and the tactician Turenne, with making Louis XIV's army the best in Europe.

## masochist

One who derives pleasure from being physically or psychologically hurt, named for German writer Leopold von Sacher-Masoch (1836–1895), who demonstrated this trait in both his novels and his own life.

## maudlin

An unwarranted display of tears and weepy sadness, named for Mary Magdalene ("maudlin" is a corruption of "Magdalene"), who is frequently depicted in art with eyes red from weeping.

## maverick

A nonconformer, someone who refuses to accept the majority opinion of the group to which he belongs, named for Samuel A. Maverick (1803–1870), Texas cattleman. Maverick's calves, left un-branded, were rounded up and appropriated by his neighbors. Hence "maverick" was used by cattlemen for any unbranded and straying animal, and from there it came to be applied to recalcitrant human beings.

## mentor

A trusted adviser or teacher, particularly a senior one, named for the wise old tutor Odysseus left behind to educate his son Telemachus.

## mercurial

An adjective used chiefly of emotions, said to be rapidly changing and flighty, named for Mercury, the Roman god of travel, commerce, and thievery, usually depicted wearing a broad-brimmed hat and sandals.

## mesmerize

To hypnotize or fascinate, named for the Austrian physician Franz Anton Mesmer (1734–1815), who pioneered the art of using the power of suggestion to cure ailments.

Mesmer never wholly understood his own technique and called it "animal magnetism" because he thought it worked by means of magnets and iron rods. Forced to leave Vienna, he took refuge in Paris in 1778, where his theories were investigated by the Academy of Science. The committee, which included the chemist Antoine Lavoisier, Dr. Joseph

Guillotin, and Benjamin Franklin, issued a negative report, and Mesmer retired to obscurity. It was only in the late-nineteenth century that scientists rediscovered mesmerism and renamed it hypnotism.

## micawber

A dreamy and improvident optimist, who relies on a change of luck to rescue him from misfortune, named for the fictional Wilkins Micawber in Charles Dickens' *David Copperfield*.

Micawber, who went through life predicting that "something will turn up," seems to have been based on Dickens' own ineffectual father.

## Midas touch

A talent for succeeding at almost any enterprise, named for the mythical king of Phrygia, who was granted the magical gift of turning things to gold by simply touching them. Since food and drink also turned to gold at his touch, Midas nearly starved to death before he begged the god Dionysus to take back his gift.

## miles gloriosus

A pompous and swaggering soldier, named for the leading character in Plautus' Latin comedy *Miles Gloriosus* ("Boastful Soldier").

## Milquetoast

An excessively meek or unassertive person, named for Caspar Milquetoast in Harold T. Webster's cartoon series "The Timid Soul."

Milk toast, an invalid food consisting of toast soaked in milk, is well-nigh tasteless.

## momus

A carping faultfinder, named for Momus, the Greek god of blame and ridicule.

## myrmidon

A faithful and unquestioning follower, named for a mythical people of Thessaly who followed their king, Achilles, to the Trojan War. Their name is derived from the Greek word for "ant" (*myrmyx*), for their ancestress was seduced by Zeus, who appeared to her in the form of an ant.

## namby-pamby

Feeble, ineffectual, named for the nickname of Ambrose Philips (1675–1749), English poet. Although the name had been conferred on Philips originally by poet Henry Carey, it was made famous by Alexander Pope, who used it of Philips during the course of a literary feud.

## Napoleonic

An adjective used in several different ways, comparing someone to one or another characteristic of the Little Corporal, named for Emperor Napoleon I (1769–1821). Someone is said to be "napoleonic" if he is short and stocky, as the emperor was, if he is excessively and greedily loyal to his family, if he desires power (in business or politics), and if he is inordinately ambitious.

## narcissism

A Freudian term for self-admiration carried to extremes, named for the mythical youth Narcissus. Loved by the nymph Echo, whom he spurned (she faded away until there was nothing left but her voice), he was punished by the goddess Nemesis by becoming so enamored of his own image that he could do nothing but sit and gaze at his reflection in a pond. Ultimately he was changed into the flower.

## Neronian

An adjective used of someone tyrannical, mean, or morally corrupt, named for the Roman Emperor Nero (A.D. 37–68). Nero—in full,

Nero Claudius Drusus Germanicus—ruled the empire for fourteen years, during which time he maintained his position by murder (notably his mother, stepbrother, and two wives), competed in festivals as actor, athlete, poet, and singer, and blamed the great fire of A.D. 64 on the Christians, whom he persecuted. Declared a public enemy by the state, he committed suicide at the age of thirty-one.

## Nestor

A greatly respected and worldly wise old man, named for Nestor in the *Iliad*, the oldest and wisest of the Greeks.

## Oedipus complex

A Freudian term for sexual attraction of a male child for his mother, named for the mythical king of Thebes, who unwittingly slew his father and married his mother. It is the opposite of the Electra complex.

## orphic

Mystic or entrancing, named for the mythical Greek poet and singer Orpheus.

When his beloved wife Eurydice died, Orpheus followed her down to the lower world, and his music so entranced even Hades, the god of the dead, that he allowed the girl to leave—on condition that Orpheus not look back at her. But the singer disobeyed, and Eurydice was forced to return forever to Hades.

## panderer

A procurer or pimp, named for the fictional Pandare in Chaucer's narrative poem *Troilus and Criseyde*. Pandare was the go-between in the love affair of the Trojan prince Troilus and the faithless Greek girl Criseyde.

## panjandrum

An important and pompous official, named for a nonsense name coined by English playwright Samuel Foote (1720–1777). Actor Charles

Mecklin had boasted to Foote that he could remember any lines of a play after hearing them once, so Foote, hoping to trip him, wrote the following:

> . . . and there were present the Picninnies, and the Loblil-lies, and the Garyalies, and the Great Panjandrum himself with the little round button at top.

## Pavlovian

Pertaining to an automatic conditioned reflex, named for Ivan Pavlov (1849–1936), Russian physiologist, whose famed experiments with dogs proved that such reflexes could be artificially produced.

In 1904 Pavlov won the Nobel Prize for medicine, for his work on the physiology of digestion.

## Pecksniffian

Sanctimonious, hypocritically pious, named for the fictional Seth Pecksniff, hateful character in Charles Dickens' *Martin Chuzzlewit.*

## peeping Tom

Someone who covertly and lasciviously watches others for the sake of an unwholesome sexual thrill, named for the tailor in eleventh-century Coventry who took an unauthorized peek at Lady Godiva.

Godiva, countess of Mercia, had begged her husband the earl to relieve the people of a certain tax, which he jestingly agreed to do if she would ride naked through the streets of Coventry. She agreed, rode naked (covered only by her long hair), and out of respect the citizens all looked the other way—except Tom the tailor, who as punishment for his temerity was struck blind.

## Penelope

A faithful wife, named for Odysseus' wife Penelope, who remained loyal throughout his twenty-year absence, holding off a drove of suitors with cunning and trickery.

## pettifogger

Someone, usually an attorney, who argues over meaningless details, probably named for the Fugger family of financiers. The Fuggers, originally of Bavarian Swabia, were descendants of an Augsburg weaver, who made themselves rich in the fifteenth and sixteenth centuries by lending money to kings.

## Philistine

A crass and vulgar materialist, named for the Philistines of ancient Palestine.

## Pied Piper

Someone who deludes his followers with enticing (and unfulfillable) promises, named for the principal character in Robert Browning's narrative poem, "The Pied Piper of Hamelin."

Based on an old German legend (which may have been based on an actual incident that took place in 1284), Browning's poem tells the story of a magician who offers to rid the city of Hamelin of its plague of rats. When the citizens refuse to pay him the sum they had agreed upon, the piper, in revenge, lures away all the children in the city.

It is thought that the tale may be a folk memory of the Children's Crusade of 1212, in which twenty thousand deluded youngsters, led by a child from Cologne, set out to fight the infidels, and instead were killed and/or enslaved.

## platonic love

A spiritual, nonphysical attraction, usually between a man and a woman, named for the Greek philosopher Plato (428–347 B.C.), who taught such a concept.

## podsnappery

A refusal to acknowledge the existence of a disagreeable situation, named for the fictional Mr. Podsnap in Charles Dickens' *Our Mutual Friend*.

## Pollyanna

An unrealistically optimistic and cheerful person, who finds good in everyone indiscriminately, named for the main character in Eleanor Porter's 1913 novel *Pollyanna*. Pollyanna was called the Glad Girl, because she always found something to be glad about in everything that happened, often beyond rational judgment.

## Pooh-Bah

A pompous government official, usually one who holds more than one office simultaneously, named for the haughty Lord-High-Everything-Else in Gilbert and Sullivan's comic opera, *The Mikado*.

## Prince Charming

Any attractive and desirable young suitor, named for the hero of Charles Perrault's famous fairy tale "Cinderella."

## procrustean

An adjective applied to arbitrary and ruthlessly enforced conformity, named for the mythical Procrustes. A giant and thief, Procrustes had a bed to which he forced all passersby to fit. If they were too short, he stretched them, and if they were too tall, he cut off their legs.

## Pygmalionism

Sexual attraction to a statue or other work of art, named for Pygmalion, the Cypriote sculptor of myth, who fell in love with his own creation—the ivory statue of a woman. At his prayer, Aphrodite brought the girl to life and named her Galatea.

## Queen of Sheba

Any woman dressed up in her best finery, named for the biblical queen who is said to have visited King Solomon about 950 B.C.:

And she came to Jerusalem with a very great train, with
camels that bare spices, and very much gold, and precious
stones: and when she was come to Solomon, she communed
with him of all that was in her heart. (I Kings 10:2)

Sheba (now called Saba) is located in modern Yemen and lies on the
India–African trade route. Following Solomon's answers to the riddles
the queen proposed to him, she complimented him profusely. According to an Arab tradition, the pair married and had children, who
eventually migrated to Ethiopia.

## quixotic

An adjective applied to an act of impractical romanticism or a person
given to such acts, named for the fictional Don Quixote in Miguel de
Cervantes' satiric *Don Quijote de la Mancha*.

The hero, an aging scholar, thinks himself a noble knight errant of the
Middle Ages, and travels about seeking adventures. No other novel has
had as many translations or reprints.

## quisling

A traitor who aids an invader in the conquering of his own country,
named for Vidkun Abraham Quisling of Norway. In 1940, Quisling, a
Nazi, helped the Germans invade and subdue his country, and in return
they made him its political head. At war's end, Quisling was tried and
executed by his countrymen.

## Rabelaisian

Characterized by coarse and earthy humor, named for the French
satirist François Rabelais (1494–1553). In his masterpiece *Gargantua
and Pantagruel*, Rabelais comments boisterously on life in sixteenth-
century France.

## ragamuffin

A ragged and dirty child, named for Ragamoffyn, a demon in William

Langland's allegorical satire "The Vision of William Concerning Piers Plowman."

## Rip Van Winkle

Someone hopelessly behind the times, named for Washington Irving's fictional character who fell asleep for twenty years. Rip, a ne'er-do-well, goes off hunting, falls in with the ghosts of Henry Hudson's crewmen, who invite him to drink from their magic keg, and afterward goes to sleep. When he wakes up, it is a different world, for Rip slept right through the Revolution, his wife is dead, his daughter grown and married, and his village unrecognizable.

## Robinson Crusoe

A castaway or someone who survives alone under trying conditions, named for Daniel Defoe's fictional hero in *The Life and Strange Surprising Adventures of Robinson Crusoe.*

Loosely based on the true adventures of Alexander Selkirk, a sailor who in 1709 was rescued from the island of Juan Fernandez, off the coast of Chile, the novel tells of Crusoe's survival of a shipwreck and subsequent attempts to feed, clothe, and shelter himself alone. (See *man Friday.*)

## rodomontade

Empty bluster and boasting, named for the fictional Rodomonte, a bragging Moorish king of Algiers in Matteo Boiardo's epic *Orlando Innamorato.*

## Romeo

A man who makes a career of lovemaking, named for the hero of Shakespeare's drama of ill-fated love, *Romeo and Juliet.*

## Rorschach test

A psychological test based on a subject's interpretation of ten inkblot designs, named for its developer Hermann Rorschach (1844–1922), a

Swiss psychiatrist. The images or pictures that the subject "sees" in the inkblots give clues to his personality.

Ironically, Dr. Rorschach's nickname as a child translates into English as "inkblot."

## sadist

One who derives satisfaction, often sexual, from inflicting mental or physical pain on others, named for Comte Donatien Alphonse François de Sade, usually called the marquis de Sade (1740–1814).

Notorious for his obscene and perverted cruelty, he was sent to Charenton Lunatic Asylum in 1789 and died there in 1814.

The word "sadist," like the word "masochist," was coined by Baron Richard von Krafft-Ebing, German neurologist who wrote extensively on sexual perversion.

## good Samaritan

Someone who goes out of his way to give aid or assistance to a person in trouble, especially in the course of a journey, named for the good neighbor of the biblical parable:

> But a certain Samaritan, as he journeyed, came where he was: and when he saw him, he had compassion on him, and went to him, and bound up his wounds, pouring in oil and wine, and set him on his own beast, and brought him to an inn, and took care of him. (Luke 10:30 ff)

The people of Samaria, a district in ancient Palestine, were considered foreigners by the Judeans and looked down upon. In the parable, however, Jesus described how the plight of the traveler, robbed and injured by thieves, was ignored by other passersby, and it was only the stranger from Samaria who took pity upon him. And in this fashion, he defined for his listener the role of the good neighbor.

## Sarah Bernhardt

Any woman with a flair for the dramatic, named for the great French actress who dominated the theater from the 1870's to the 1920's. Born Henriette Rosine Bernard (1844–1923), the "Divine Sarah" possessed an exceptional speaking voice plus a commanding theatrical technique, which permitted her to continue her acting career even after a 1914 leg amputation.

## sardonic

Mocking, humorously derisive, sneering, named for *Sardonia herba* (the Sardinian herb), a poisonous plant thought to make those who eat it insane, because it distorted their facial features.

## satanic

Diabolical, evil, named for the archfiend of the Bible. The name itself is derived from the Hebrew *shatan* ("adversary"), and is mentioned in both Old and New Testaments:

> And the Lord said unto Satan, Behold, all that he hath is in thy power; only upon himself put not forth thine hand. So Satan went forth from the presence of the Lord. (Job 1:12) And Jesus answered and said unto him, Get thee behind me, Satan: for it is written, Thou shalt worship the Lord thy God and him only shalt thou serve. (Luke 4:8)

## saturnine

Morose, cynical, named for Saturn, the Roman god of agriculture and the planet named for him. Astrologists traditionally associated sluggishness and glum humor with the planet's influence.

Ironically, the ancient Roman festival of Saturn, beginning December 17, called the Saturnalia, was a period of wild revelry, with an exchange of gifts, feasting, and sexual permissiveness—perhaps a forerunner of the more spiritual Christian feast of Christmas.

## scalawag

A rascal, rapscallion, someone naughty (often used humorously or affectionately), named for the village of Scallaway on Mainland Isiand, Shetland Islands, Scotland.

Originally the term meant a runtish animal, like the small Shetland ponies; later it came to apply to small-time crooks, and eventually it was used as a term for a Southern Republican during Reconstruction.

## scapegoat

A person or thing who carries the blame for another's mistakes or misdeeds, named for a mistranslation of the Hebrew Azazel, the name of a demon. Translators read this as *ez ozel*, "departing goat," and rendered it into English as "scapegoat."

The mistake was all the easier to make since the reference is to an actual goat which was used during the solemn Hebrew Day of Atonement. The sins of the people were symbolically placed on the head of a goat, which was then allowed to escape into the desert. The Bible states that the high priest Aaron

> . . . shall take of the congregation of the children of Israel two kids of the goats for a sin offering . . . And Aaron shall cast lots upon the two goats; one lot for the Lord, and the other lot for the scapegoat. (Leviticus 16:5–10)

## schlemiel

A born loser, clumsy and naive, named for the biblical prince of Simeon, Shelumiel, who lost battles while other Hebrew generals were winning them.

## Scrooge

A grasping and miserly person, named for the fictional Ebenezer Scrooge in Charles Dickens' *A Christmas Carol*.

## shylock

A usurer, a loan shark, one who lends out money at extortionate rates of interests, named for the fictional Shylock in Shakespeare's *The Merchant of Venice*. Shylock lent money to Antonio, demanding in return for nonpayment a pound of the merchant's flesh. The term "a pound of flesh" has similarly become synonymous with demands for an excessive return in someone's time or effort.

## sibyl

A female prophet or fortune-teller, named for the Sibyls of the ancient world, said to be two to twelve in number. The best known was the Cumaean Sybil, who dwelt in a cave at Cumae, on the Italian shore west of Naples, and is said to have prophesied to Aeneas the founding of Rome.

## Simon Legree

A demanding taskmaster, a boss who makes unreasonable demands for work (often used humorously), named for the fictional slave owner in Harriet Beecher Stowe's novel *Uncle Tom's Cabin*. In the novel the cruel Simon eventually flogs the slave Tom to death.

The book, published in 1852, sold 300,000 copies its first year, a phenomenal sale for the period, and was credited by President Lincoln with helping to bring on the American Civil War.

## Simple Simon

A gullible person, easily victimized, named for the nursery-rhyme pieman.

## Solomon

A wise person, named for the biblical King Solomon, son of David and Bathsheba, who ruled Israel in the tenth century B.C. and was renowned for his judgment.

His most famous mediation concerned the dispute of two women over which one was the true mother of a child.

> And the king said, Bring me a sword. And they brought a sword before the king. And the king said, Divide the living child in two, and give half to the one, and half to the other. (I Kings 3:24–25)

The true mother backed down and agreed to let the other keep the child, and the king therefore recognized her and gave the child to her.

## Solon

A wise lawgiver, especially one who lays down principles of law, named for the Greek lawgiver who reformed the laws of Athens in the sixth century B.C.

Solon, considered one of the Seven Wise Men of ancient Greece, eased the harsh laws of Draco, improved the lot of debtors, and reorganized the ruling forms of government, then went into voluntary exile for ten years to give the new system time to be tried out.

## spartan

Characterized by simplicity, self-discipline, and lack of comforts, named for the ancient city of Sparta, whose citizens lived a life devoted to rigorous military training.

Most city-states of mountainous Greece were protected by hills, whose narrow passes could be easily defended by citizen militiamen, but Sparta lay in an open plain, its only protection the bodies of its soldiers. Therefore, all education and life-style were devoted to building and supporting an army of soldiers, drilled to survive the harshest hardships.

## Sphinx

A person of enigmatic character, a mystery woman (or man), named for the monster of Greek mythology who had the body of a winged lion and the face of a woman and destroyed all passersby who could not answer her riddle:

> What is it that walks on four feet in the morning, on two feet at noon, and three feet in the evening?

Oedipus escaped death by correctly answering that it was man—who crawled as an infant, walked erect in adulthood, and used a cane in old age. The monster then committed suicide.

The famous five-thousand-year-old Sphinx of Egypt, although it was named by the Greeks, has no relationship to the mythological monster. Built by King Khephren out of a 239-foot block of limestone, it has the body of a lion (representing royal power) and the king's face. Because it faces the rising sun, it has come to be regarded as a sun god.

## splacknuck

A person or animal of odd appearance or personality, named for the fictional Splacknuck, an animal in Jonathan Swift's *Gulliver's Travels*.

## Svengali

One who controls the actions of another for his own advantage, named for the evil hypnotist in George du Maurier's novel *Trilby*. Svengali mesmerized the Irish girl Trilby into becoming a great singer, but after his death, she lost her voice and her career.

## sybarite

One whose principal goal in life is enjoying voluptuous pleasures, named for the ancient city of Sybaris (near modern Terranova di Sibari, Italy), famed for the self-indulgence of its inhabitants.

## tantalize

To torment someone by awakening desire and then frustrating it, named for Tantalus, the king of ancient Phrygia.

For behaving toward the gods with overbearing ingratitude, Tantalus was condemned to eternal punishment in Tartarus. Suffering from unappeased hunger and thirst, he was forced to stand in water up to his chin while the finest fruits hung from branches over his head. Whenever he opened his mouth to eat or drink, the water dried up and the fruits vanished.

## Tartuffe

A hypocrite, especially one who pretends piety, named for the fictional religious imposter in Molière's comedy *Tartuffe* (1664).

## tartar

An unexpectedly strong or fierce-tempered individual, named for the Mongol hordes who swept into eastern Europe in the thirteenth century under Genghis Khan. "To catch a tartar" is to find oneself struggling with an opponent who is extremely hard to handle.

## titan

One who stands out above the crowd, named for the mythological earth giants called Titans. The six sons and six daughters of Uranus and Gaea, of whom the most famous was Cronus, father of Zeus, the Titans were characterized by brute strength, large size, and low intelligence.

They revolted against their father and set up Cronus as the ruler of the world, and he in turn was overthrown by his son, who established the rule of the Olympian gods.

The adjective "titanic" is applied to things of immense size and strength.

## Tommy Atkins

A typical British soldier, the English equivalent of the American "GI Joe," named for the Duke of Wellington's soldier-servant, whose name he borrowed to use as a model in filling in blank forms.

## Turk

An unfeeling tyrant (often used humorously), named for the warlike people of the east who conquered the Byzantine Empire and established their own in its place, the Ottoman Empire.

## Uncle Tom

A black man who humbles himself obsequiously before whites, named for the leading character in Harriet Beecher Stowe's *Uncle Tom's Cabin*.

## vandal

One who wantonly damages or destroys property, named for the Vandals, a Germanic people, who in A.D. 455 invaded Italy and plundered Rome.

## vestal

A woman of rigid purity who remains chaste usually by choice, named for the Vestal Virgins of ancient Rome, young women devoted to the service of Vesta, goddess of the hearth.

It was a great honor to be named a Vestal Virgin. Chosen at the age of between six and ten, a girl served in the temple of Vesta for a period that ranged from five to thirty years, tending the sacred fire and preparing sacrifices. Vestals were given the best seats at public spectacles and were preceded by public attendants when they walked abroad, but if they failed to remain chaste during their time of service, they could be burned or entombed alive.

## Victorian

Characterized by stuffiness, hypocrisy, or excessively rigid morals, named for the period in England in which Queen Victoria reigned, when social repression was widespread.

## Xanthippe

A bad-tempered, shrewish woman, named for Xanthippe, the wife of Socrates, reputedly a nagging scold.

## Yahoo

A crude, disorderly lout, named for the Yahoos, a fictional race of brutes in Jonathan Swift's *Gulliver's Travels*.

## Young Turk

A member of a rebellious group within a larger group, which wants to take control of it for the sake of reform, named for the insurgents against the Ottoman Empire who called themselves the Young Turk Committee of Union and Progress. In 1908 they forced the government to accept a reform constitution.

# The Body:
# All Sizes and Shapes

Nature has blessed the world with a grand variety of individuals and groups. Their heterogeneity is reflected in the words we use to describe them and their component parts.

## BODY TYPES . . .

### Adonis

A very handsome young man, named for the mythological youth Adonis. Both Aphrodite, goddess of love, and Persephone, queen of the underworld, fell in love with Adonis. When he was killed in a boar hunt, Aphrodite changed him into an anemone, and thereafter Zeus decreed he was to spend one half of each year with Aphrodite (spring and summer) and the other half with Persephone (fall and winter).

### gargantuan

Enormous, huge, named for Gargantua, the kingly hero of Rabelais' satiric novel *Gargantua and Pantagruel*.

Gargantua was so large that, even as an infant, he consumed daily the milk of 17,913 cows and had his hair combed by a nine-hundred-foot-long rake. In later years he spat out teeth that became boulders and hills, and his urine became rivers and lakes.

## Goliath

An adjective meaning large and strong, named for the biblical giant Goliath, the Philistine champion.

For forty days, Goliath challenged the Israelis to choose a champion to fight him, and finally David, a shepherd boy, accepted. Armed with a sling and five smooth stones, he went out to fight his nine-feet-tall adversary.

> And David put his hand in his bag, and took thence a stone, and slang it, and smote the Philistine in his forehead, that the stone sunk into his forehead; and he fell upon his face to the earth. (I Samuel 17:49).

## herculean

An adjective meaning possessing great strength, named for the mythical hero Hercules.

The son of Zeus and Alcmene, Hercules (Heracles in Greek) murdered his three children in a fit of madness and in punishment was condemned to perform twelve tasks of superhuman difficulty. The Twelve Labors of Hercules were the slaying of the Nemean lion, the beheading of the hydra of Lerna, the capture of the Erymanthean boar, the wounding of the Arcadian hind, the dispersing of the Stymphalian birds, the theft of Hippolyte's girdle, the cleaning of the Augean stables, the capture of the Cretan bull, the capture of the mares of Diomedes, the seizure of the cattle of Geryon, the plucking of the golden apples of the Hesperides, and the kidnapping of Cerberus, the guard dog of the underworld.

## Humpty-Dumpty

Something esoteric and fragile, which once shattered cannot be restored to its original function, named for the nursery-rhyme character who fell off a wall.

The term "Humpty-Dumpty" can also be used to describe someone short and round, since the original was egg-shaped.

## Methuselah

A very old man, named for the biblical Methuselah, who supposedly lived 769 years.

## Samson

One who has great physical strength, named for Samson, an Israelite judge, renowned for his power. Betrayed by his beloved Delilah, he was blinded and set to grinding corn for the Philistines, and in revenge he broke the pillars of the temple and brought the roof crashing down on his enemies.

The term "Samson post" is used to describe any chief supporting member, particularly that which rests on a ship's keelson and holds up the deck beams.

## Tom Thumb

Any person or thing of very small stature, named for the legendary folk hero who was supposedly no bigger than his father's thumb.

A real-life Tom Thumb, Charles Sherwood Stratton (1838–1883), was somewhat bigger. Born of normal parents, Stratton stood three feet four inches tall and married a woman midget slightly taller than he. Both were stars of P.T. Barnum's museum of freaks, where they were billed as General and Mrs. Tom Thumb.

## Venus

A beautiful, very feminine woman, named for the Roman goddess of love. Venus was married to Vulcan, god of fire and metalworking, and the mother of Cupid (desire) and Hymen (marriage).

# BODY PARTS . . .

## Achilles heel

A strong tendon that runs from the calf of the leg to the heel, named for mythological Achilles, who was invulnerable everywhere except at that one point. His mother, who dipped him into the River Styx to render him immortal, held him by the heel, and since this one spot was untouched by the water, it was here that he received his mortal wound.

By extension "Achilles heel" is used to mean one's vulnerable or weak point.

## Adam's apple

A slight bulge in the throat, more prominent in males than in females, caused by the thyroid cartilage, named for the biblical Adam. In the book of Genesis, Eve gave Adam the forbidden fruit of the tree of knowledge of good and evil (in popular terms, "the apple"), and for this sin, they were cast out of the Garden of Eden.

## Eustachian tube

A duct connecting the middle ear with the rear of the throat, named for its discoverer Bartolommeo Eustachio (1524–1574), an Italian anatomist.

## Fallopian tubes

The oviducts found in female mammals, including human beings, where fertilization of the egg takes place, named for Gabriello Fallopio (1523–1562), Italian anatomist. The term "tubes" is a mistranslation of Fallopio's *tubas*, "trumpets," which was his way of describing the horn-shaped organs.

Fallopio also described the clitoris, showed that virgins have hymens, and coined the word "vagina." His name has also been applied to the facial canal, a uterine ligament, and several other anatomical structures.

## hymen

A membranous tissue that covers the vaginal opening, named for the Greek god of marriage, who was invoked at wedding ceremonies.

## iris

The "color" part of the eye, named for Iris, the Greek goddess of the rainbow. The iris of the eye has a center opening called the pupil, which is round in human beings and some animals, vertically slit in cats, and horizontally slit in goats.

"Iris" is also another name for the flower known as flag or flower-de-luce (fleur-de-lis).

# HEALERS OF THE SICK . . .

## Hippocratic Oath

An oath to uphold medical ethics, taken by most physicians at the time they are granted their M.D. degrees, named for Hippocrates of Cos (460–377 B.C.), the Father of Medicine.

## hygiene

The science of establishing and maintaining good health, named for Hygeia, the Greek goddess of health. Hygeia was the daughter of Aesculapius and is often pictured feeding a pet snake, the symbol of rejuvenescence.

## lazaretto

A hospital for contagious diseases, or pest house, probably named for the biblical beggar Lazarus. In Luke 16:20, he is described only as being "full of sores," but this has usually been interpreted to mean that he was a leper.

# DISEASES OF HUMANKIND . . .

## Bilharziasis

A tropical disease caused by parasitic worms, transmitted by aquatic snails, named for Theodor Bilharz (1825–1858), the German parasitologist who discovered the disease and described its cause.

## Bright's disease

A destructive form of kidney disease, named for its discoverer, Richard Bright (1789–1858), an English physician.

## brucellosis

Undulant fever, a disease of men and animals, caused by an organism of the genus Brucella, named for bacteriologist Sir David Bruce (1855–1931).

A specialist in tropical diseases, Dr. Bruce also discovered the cause of nagana (trypanosomiasis), sleeping sickness, Mediterranean fever, and other disorders endemic in Africa.

## Chagas disease

Trypanosomiasis of tropical America, transmitted by a variety of bloodsucking insects, named for Carlos Chagas (1879–1934), a Brazilian physician, who discovered it in 1909.

The son of a coffee planter, Dr. Chagas unearthed the secrets of this disease while working to eradicate malaria. He labored over Chagas disease for two years, living in a railroad car in a remote village, and ultimately was able to describe the entire history of the disease from identification of the causative agent on through to treatment of the symptoms—the only time in medical history when one investigator has dealt with all phases of a malady.

## Charcot's disease

Multiple sclerosis, a disease of the central nervous system, named for Jean Martin Charcot (1825–1893), French neurologist, who distinguished it from the similar affliction paralysis agitans.

The son of a French wheelwright, Charcot in time became world-famed for his neurological studies and attracted such important pupils as Sigmund Freud. He was often innovative in his presentation of clinical findings and sometimes had patients present their symptoms on the public stage. In 1867 he published a book on old age, an important beginning in the field of geriatric medicine.

## Coxsackie virus

A viral disease similar to polio but without paralysis, named for the Hudson Valley town of Coxsackie, New York. The virus was first recognized in the bloodstream of a resident of Coxsackie.

## Cushing's syndrome

A disease of the adrenal cortex, characterized by obesity, muscular weakness, and porosity of bone, named for Harvey W. Cushing (1869–1939), American neurologist. Cushing, one of the founders of neurosurgery and a pioneer in operations on the pituitary gland, described the etiology of the condition from firsthand knowledge.

Cushing not only wrote medical reports but illustrated them as well. In 1926 he won the Pulitzer Prize for a biography of Sir William Osler, famous English clinician.

## Daltonism

Red-green color blindness, named for John Dalton (1766–1844), English chemist and physicist, who was the first to investigate this condition. He was prompted to the study when his friends mentioned that his clothes did not match, and he realized that, although he could distinguish yellow, purple, and blue, he could not tell red from green.

Dalton also formulated the first atomic theory and devised the first table of atomic weights, identified the aurora borealis as an electrical discharge, and determined the law of partial pressures, which is known as Dalton's law.

## Hansen's disease

Leprosy, named for Dr. Armauer Hansen (1841–1912), Norwegian physician, who discovered the organism that causes this dread disease.

As a medical officer for the Norwegian government, he helped bring about improvements in the treatment of leprosy, although it was not until after the discovery of sulfa drugs in the 1940's that dramatic strides were made in arresting the progress of the disease.

## Hodgkin's disease

A tumorous disease of the lymph glands, spleen, and liver, named for Thomas Hodgkin (1798–1866), English physician, who first described the condition.

## Legionnaires' disease

A viral form of pneumonia, named for members of the American Legion, who were the first to suffer from an outbreak of the disease. Having assembled for a convention in Philadelphia in the summer of 1976, the legionnaires had dispersed to their homes before the outbreak caught the public attention. Before the epidemic died down, 179 people had contracted the disease, and twenty-eight were dead.

## mongolism

Congenital retardation, characterized by eyes that appear to slant and named for this Oriental characteristic. Modern doctors prefer to call the condition Down's syndrome, after J.L.H. Down, nineteenth-century English physician, who described it.

## Parkinson's disease

Shaking palsy (a literal translation of the Latin name *paralysis agitans*), named for James Parkinson (1755–1824), English surgeon, who described this condition in a paper he published in 1817, *An Essay on the Shaking Palsy*.

Parkinson was also the first to write about the disease appendicitis. As an M.P. he spoke out in Parliament on behalf of universal suffrage, improved health care for the common people, and protection of the rights of the confined insane.

## Rickettsia

A genus of microorganisms carried by ticks, fleas, and lice and causing such diseases as typhus, Rocky Mountain spotted fever, heartwater (a disease of sheep, goats and cattle), and rickettsialpox, named for Howard T. Ricketts (1871–1910), American pathologist, who discovered them.

Rickettsia are intermediate in size between the relatively large bacteria and the relatively tiny viruses. Like the bacteria (but not viruses) rickettsia are often successfully combated by antibiotics.

## St. Vitus' dance

Chorea, a nervous disorder characterized by involuntary uncontrollable movements of the body, named for a boy Christian supposedly martyred during Diocletian's reign. Vitus is the patron saint of epileptics, victims of rabies, and those suffering from nervous disorders.

The technical name of the affliction, "chorea," is derived from the Greek word for "dance."

## Salmonella

A genus of bacteria associated chiefly with food poisoning and diseases of the genital tract, named for Daniel E. Salmon (1850–1914), a veterinarian with the Bureau of Animal Industry, U.S. Department of Agriculture. Salmon organized meat-inspecting systems, established quarantine periods for livestock imported from abroad, and instigated techniques for suppressing contagious diseases of cattle.

## saturnism

Lead poisoning, named for the planet Saturn, associated astrologically with lead.

## tularemia

An infectious disease of men, rodents, and certain domestic animals, named for Tulare County, California, where it was first discovered in 1912 in ground squirrels. Men usually contract the disease by handling infected wild animals.

### Vincent's angina

Trenchmouth, an infection of tonsils, pharynx, and throat, named for French bacteriologist Jean Vincent (1862–1950), who discovered the bacteria producing it.

Dr. Vincent, educated as an army doctor, first noticed the disease among soldiers serving in trenches. He also developed vaccines for typhoid and paratyphoid and a serum for gas gangrene.

### Winchester goose

A venereal disease that causes groinal swelling, named for the bishop of Winchester, who had jurisdiction over an area in which there were a number of brothels.

# • PREVENTIONS AND CURES •

## TESTS AND VACCINES

### Dick test

An intracutaneous injection to determine susceptibility or immunity to scarlet fever, named for the husband-and-wife team who developed it, George (1881–1967) and Gladys (1881–1963) Dick.

### Pap smear

A test for the presence of cancer cells in the cervix, named for the Greek-born American physician who developed it, George Nicholas Papanicolaou (1883–1962). Pap tests have been credited with saving thousands of women's lives by detecting the disease early in its treatable stage.

### Sabin vaccine

Live-virus vaccine against poliomyelitis, taken by mouth, named for its developer Albert Bruce Sabin (b. 1906), a Polish-born American Jew. Dr. Sabin first tried out his oral vaccine on himself before he allowed volunteers to test it. In use around the world, the Sabin vaccine has virtually wiped out polio.

### Salk vaccine

Killed-virus vaccine against poliomyelitis, taken by injection, named for its developer Jonas Edward Salk (b. 1914). Dr. Salk, son of an immigrant Polish-Jewish garment worker, was the first man in history to find a way to immunize people against crippling polio. By the time Dr. Sabin's vaccine came along, two years later, there was little need for it in the United States—the Salk vaccine had done the job. In ten years the two together caused a drop in cases from 21,000 in 1952 to 893 in 1962. In the 1970's, five cases per year are considered an epidemic.

### Schick test

An intracutaneous injection to test susceptibility or immunity to diphtheria, named for its developer Bèla Schick (1877–1967). Hungarian-born Dr. Schick was pediatrician-in-chief for many years at New York's famed Mount Sinai Hospital.

# MEDICINES

### bacitracin

An antibiotic, chiefly used in external salves, named for Margaret Tracy, a young American in whose blood it was first isolated in 1945.

### bougie

A taper-shaped suppository, named for the seaport city of Bougie (now Bejaïa), Algeria, from which fine wax candles were once exported.

## Calabar bean

The seed of a tropical African vine, named for the town of Calabar, Nigeria, from which it is exported. Though Calabar bean is itself poisonous, useful alkaloids can be extracted from it for such uses as causing the pupil of the eye to contract.

## calamine lotion

A pink substance of zinc and ferric oxide, used in lotions and ointments, whose name is a corruption of Cadmean. Zinc (Cadmean earth) was first mined near Thebes, a city founded by the mythical hero Cadmus.

## carron oil

A solution of linseed oil and limewater, named for the ironworks at Carron, Scotland, whose workers were treated for burns with this compound.

## chalybeate

An adjective meaning "mixed with iron," used chiefly of water drunk as medicine, named for the Chalybes, ancient metalworkers of Asia Minor, who are credited with discovering how to work iron.

## Dakin's fluid

A solution of sodium hypochlorite used as a surgical disinfectant, named for British chemist Henry Drysdale Dakin (1880–1952), who developed it during World War I.

## Dover's powder

A compound of ipecac and opium, used to induce perspiration and relieve pain, named for its discoverer Thomas Dover (1660–1742). Dover, an Englishman, a physician, and a captain of a privateer, combined his medical and nautical abilities to cure 172 of his crewmen of an illness.

## Epsom salts

A crystalline salt of magnesium sulfate heptahydrate, named for the magnesium springs discovered around 1618 in the vicinity of Epsom in Surrey, England. Epsom salts are used both internally as a laxative and externally as a soaking aid for bruises, sprains, and local inflammations.

## Glauber's salts

Hydrated sodium sulfate, used as a laxative and named for the German chemist and physician Johann Rudolf Glauber (1604–1668), who did much early experimenting with salts.

Glauber, the son of a barber and author of some forty books dealing with the use of chemistry in industry, altruistically devoted one hour a day to dispensing free medicines to the poor.

## morphine

An alkaloid, habit-forming narcotic derived from opium and named for Morpheus, the Greek god of dreams. It is sometimes used to relieve severe pain—but, because of its addictive qualities, sparingly. Heroin is, in turn, derived from morphine, but unlike the parent drug heroin has no accepted medical use.

## quassia

A substance derived from the heartwood of various tropical trees, named for the eighteenth-century black slave Graman Quassi, who discovered its medical properties in Surinam. Quassia has various uses, chiefly as a treatment for roundworm in children.

## Rauwolfia

A genus of tropical trees and shrubs, source of the tranquilizer reserpine, named for Leonhard Rauwolf, sixteenth-century German botanist.

## Seidlitz powders

A compound of effervescent powders, one of which is the familiar bicarbonate of soda, named for the Czechoslovakian village of Seidlitz (now Sedlčany), whose mineral springs produce a similar substance.

## senega

A North American milkwort whose dried root was formerly prescribed for respiratory ailments, named for the Seneca Indians of New York. The Seneca treated snakebite with senega, but today it is most commonly used as an expectorant.

## valerian

A drug derived from the dried rhizomes of the garden heliotrope (*Valeriana officinalis*), named for the Roman diocese Valeria Ripensis (now western Hungary), where the plant grew. It is used to relieve colic and as a sedative.

## Veronal

Proprietary name for a brand of barbital, named by its German developers for the sleeping potion in *Romeo and Juliet*, whose native city was Verona, Italy.

# MEDICAL TOOLS AND METHODS

## bistoury

A long, narrow surgical knife, used for opening up abscesses and fistulas, whose name is a corruption of Pistoia, an Italian town which specialized in the manufacture of sharp knives. Cutlery and needles are still important products there.

## Bunsen burner

A device for producing a small, intensely hot, gas-fed flame, for use in laboratory experiments, named for its inventor, German chemist Robert Wilhelm Bunsen (1811–1899). Bunsen also pioneered in spectrum analysis, formulated the reciprocity law, discovered the elements cesium and rubidium, and invented several other scientific devices.

## caesarian section

A surgical procedure in which an expectant mother's abdomen is opened and the baby delivered through the uterine wall, named for the ancient Roman *Lex caesarea*, which required that such an operation be performed on a dying woman to save the child.

Although the mistaken belief that Julius Caesar was born this way helped to promote the name, it is actually derived from the fact that it was established during the century and a quarter that the Caesars ruled the Roman Empire.

Today the operation is performed when it is thought that natural birth will be dangerous to mother or child.

## gauze

A thinly woven, transparent fabric used in bandages and bandage pads, named for Gaza in Palestine (now in dispute between Egypt and Israel), where the hot climate made light fabrics necessary.

## Gram's method

A technique for staining bacteria in order to facilitate their study and identification, named for its developer, Danish physician Hans Christian Joachim Gram (1853–1938). Certain bacteria retain the stain while others do not, and they are thus called respectively *gram-positive* and *gram-negative*.

## Heimlich hug

A method of dislodging food or other particles from a choking person's throat, named for its developer, Dr. Henry Heimlich. This technique, in which the rescuer encircles the victim with his arms and jabs him sharply in the solar plexus, utilizes the air remaining in the victim's own lungs to expel the particle from his windpipe.

## pasteurization

A method of heating liquids, chiefly milk, to a temperature that will kill bacteria without altering the liquid's chemical composition, named for its developer, French chemist Louis Pasteur (1822–1895). Pasteurized milk is not only safer to drink than unpasteurized but will last longer without spoiling.

## petri dish

A shallow, covered dish used to grow microorganisms for scientific research, named for Julius R. Petri, German bacteriologist and assistant to Robert Koch, who invented it.

## Valentin's knife

A double-bladed knife used to cut thin slices of tissue, named for German physiologist Gabriel Valentin (1810–1883), who invented it.

Dr. Valentin, son of a silverware merchant and assistant rabbi, was the first Jew to be granted citizenship by the city of Bern, Switzerland.

# Part 3

## OUR MATERIAL NEEDS

# · ⑥ ·

# Food: Eat, Drink and Be Merry

From the fields we plant in to the dishes we serve, a significant part of our lives is involved in the production, preparation, and consumption of food. Moreover, for as long as humanity has existed, individuals, groups and societies have contributed their cuisine and their specialties to the world's food pot—and their names to the world's vocabulary.

## BUT BEFORE WE EAT . . .

### Barmecidal

Illusory, nonexistent, especially in connection with food and dining, named for the aristocratic Barmecide family in the *Arabian Nights* tale "The Barber's Sixth Brother." In the story, the starving beggar Schacabac is served a "feast" of empty dishes by a Barmecide prince, and when he valiantly cooperates and pretends to enjoy the imaginary meal, his host relents and plies him with a real one.

### epicure

An expert in fine food and other earthly delights, named for the Greek philosopher Epicurus (341–270 B.C.) who taught that pleasure is the only good. However, by "pleasure" Epicurus meant intellectual and spiritual pursuits—justice, prudence, honor—rather than sensual, and our modern understanding of the word "epicure" is based on the misinterpretation of outsiders.

## Fletcherism

A system of diet named for its American developer, Horace Fletcher (1849–1919). Fletcherism involves eating only when hungry, eating small amounts at a time, and chewing thoroughly, eating only what appeals to you, and not eating when anxious or depressed.

Fletcher, who had long been subject to indigestion and frequent illnesses, took up this regimen after he was turned down by a life-insurance company for being fifty pounds overweight. The new system put him back in shape within four years, at which time he celebrated his fiftieth birthday with a two-hundred-mile bicycle ride.

# TABLEWARE AND COOKING UTENSILS . . .

## bain-marie ("Mary bath")

A steam table or double boiler, specifically one with a broad copper bottom and a narrower porcelain top, named for Miriam (Mary), sister of Moses and Aaron. Miriam, a prophetess, is the reputed author of a treatise on alchemy, a study that involved a good deal of heating and cooking.

## china

Vitreous porcelain ware, named for its country of origin. The Chinese began making porcelain as early as the tenth century, but Europeans did not master the art until eight hundred years later.

## delft

A blue-and-white glazed pottery, originally made in imitation of Chinese porcelain, named for the town of Delft in the Netherlands, where it was produced.

## doily

A decorative napkin or mat, usually decorated with lace or crochet work, set under a plate or vase to protect the tabletop, named for a London draper named Doyley.

## Dresden

Hard-paste porcelain, a byword for delicacy and intricate design, named for the city of Dresden, the capital of Saxony, East Germany, near which it was manufactured. Dresden china is sometimes called Meissenware from the royal porcelain factory at the town of Meissen, some miles down the Elbe River from the capital.

## gombroon

A white porcelain, named for the Iranian port city of Gombroon, from which it was shipped. Gombroon is now called Bandar Abbas in honor of its founder, Shah Abbas I (1557–1628).

## jorum

A very large drinking vessel, such as a jug or tankard, named for Joram, son of the king of Hamath (now Nahr-el-Asi, Syria), who sent him to King David with "vessels of silver, and vessels of gold, and vessels of brass" (II Samuel 8:10).

## majolica

A colorful glazed earthenware, named for the Spanish island of Majorca, where it was made.

## mason jar

A wide-topped glass jar with an airtight, screw-on lid, used for home canning, named for its American inventor John L. Mason (1832–1902).

## Sèvres

An elegant, richly decorated variety of porcelain, named for the French town of Sèvres, where it is made. Originally located in Vincennes, the factory was taken over by Louis XV in 1756 and moved to Sèvres. It was nationalized by the republican government in 1793.

## Spode

Ceramic ware manufactured at Stoke-on-Trent, England, and named for its manufacturer, Josiah Spode (1733–1797). An innovative potter, Spode developed the technique for adding bone ash to porcelain and thus producing the delicate white translucent tableware known as bone china.

## Wedgwood

Pottery made and named for Josiah Wedgwood (1730–1795), particularly pieces of classical design, white on "Wedgwood blue." Wedgwood also manufactured bone china, cream-colored queensware, various-colored jasperware, and black basalt.

Intellectual and liberal, scientific in his approach to his craft, Wedgwood associated with some of the finest minds of his day. His daughter Susannah became the mother of Charles Darwin, and his youngest son Thomas is regarded as the first to discover the principles upon which photography is based.

## Worcester china

A soft-paste porcelain, named for the city of Worcester, England, where it has been manufactured since 1751. Worcester pioneered in the art of decorating china with copperplate engraving.

# A JUG OF WINE . . .

## jeroboam

A large wine bottle, usually containing four fifths of a gallon, named for Jeroboam, king of northern Israel from 933 to 912 B.C. He is described as "a mighty man of valor" (I Kings 11:28).

## Rehoboam

A large wine bottle holding about five quarts, named for Rehoboam, the first king of southern Judah, and a son of Solomon. An enemy of Jeroboam, he revolted against his tyranny.

## Methuselah

A large wine bottle holding about six and a half quarts, named for the oldest man in the Bible.

## Nebuchadnezzar

An enormous wine bottle, holding twenty quarts, named (presumably because he was an all-powerful ruler in his day) for the king of Babylon who destroyed Jerusalem in 586 B.C.

# $H_2O$ PLUS . . .

## Adam's ale

Water, named for the chief resident of the Garden of Eden, where there was supposedly no other beverage.

## Vichy water

Soda water, named for Vichy, France, where it is found in nine alkaline springs. For centuries men have visited these springs to "take the waters" for their digestive ills. Today, in bottled form Vichy water is shipped all over the world. It is virtually identical to common supermarket bottled soda.

## seltzer

An effervescent mineral water, named for the springs from which it originally came at Nieder Selters, near Wiesbaden, West Germany. The German *Selterserwasser* ("Selters water") eventually became corrupted to *seltzer water*.

# THE HARD STUFF . . .

## Armagnac

A heady variety of brandy, made in Gascony and named for the region in southwest France where its production is centered. It is distilled in portable stills and aged in barrels of local Armagnac oak.

## Bloody Mary

A tall drink consisting of vodka, tomato juice, and seasoning, named for Queen Mary I of England, whose reign was marked by savage repression of Protestantism.

## bock beer

The first beer taken from the vats in spring, heavy and dark, named for Einbeck, West Germany. The Germans themselves corrupted *Einbeckerbier* to *Bockbier*, and since *Bock* is the German for "he-goat," bock beer is often advertised by a picture of a billy goat.

## bourbon

Whiskey distilled from corn, rye, and malted barley, named for its place of origin, Bourbon County, Kentucky. Bourbon, along with pure corn whiskey, is the only distillate invented in the United States.

## Burgundy

Red or white table wine named for the region in eastern France from which it comes. Burgundy, which lies along the western bank of the Saone River between Lyons and Auxerre, produces a heavier-bodied wine than other regions of France.

## Calvados

Apple brandy named for the department of northern France (part of ancient Normandy) where it originates.

Calvados Reef, near the Norman village of Asnelle, marks the main landing area for Allied troops on the D-Day invasion of the European mainland, June 6, 1944, lying between the central and eastern beach-heads.

## champagne

An effervescent white wine, named for the area in northeastern France where it originated. There, improved methods of winemaking were developed by monks at the end of the seventeenth century. According to French law, only champagne from the region of Champagne can carry this name on its label.

## chianti

A dry red wine named for the region where it is grown, the Chianti Mountains, a range of the Apennines in Tuscany, Italy.

## cognac

Brandy double-distilled in a pot still from a hard, acid wine, aged in casks of Limousin oak, and named for the town in east-central France near which it originated. True cognac comes only from the region watered by the Charente River.

## cuba libre

A highball made of rum, lime juice, and cola, named for the slogan of Cuban insurrectionists ("Free Cuba!") of the 1890's.

## daiquiri

A cocktail of rum, lime (or lemon), and sugar, named for the town in Oriente Province, Cuba, near which American troops landed during the Spanish-American War, June 22, 1898.

## grog

Spirits (usually rum) cut with water, named for the nickname of Admiral Edward Vernon (1684–1757), who ordered the Royal Navy's rum ration to be so diluted. Vernon was known as Old Grog from his habit of wearing, in foul weather, a cloak made of the material called grogram.

Vernon, who was much admired by George Washington's older half-brother Lawrence of Virginia, for his exploits in King George's War, also lent his name to America's most famous plantation: Mount Vernon.

## hippocras

A highly spiced wine, named for Hippocrates (460–377 B.C.), its purported inventor.

## hock

White wine from the river valleys of western Germany, chiefly Rhine and Mosel, named for the town of Hochheim on the Main, which produced a famous variety of German wine.

## hooch

Alcohol, especially if illegally made, named for the Hoochinoo Indians, a Tlingit people of Alaska, who did some moonshining.

## malmsey

A variety of sweet Madeira, made from the malvasia grape, whose name is a corruption of Monemvasia, a town in the Greek Peloponnesus, where it was first grown.

## Manhattan

Cocktail made of vermouth and whiskey, named for the island of Manhattan in New York City.

The island itself was named for the Manhattan Indians, an Algonkian-speaking people, who once inhabited it.

## negus

A hot concoction of wine, lemon juice, hot water, sugar, and nutmeg, named for an eighteenth-century English soldier who invented it, Colonel Francis Negus.

## rob roy

Cocktail made of Scotch whisky, vermouth, and bitters, named for Rob Roy ("Red Rob") MacGregor (1671–1734), Scots outlaw. A kind of one-man Cosa Nostra, who led a gang of wild Highland ruffians and sold "protection" to his neighbors, MacGregor was immortalized in Sir Walter Scott's novel *Rob Roy*.

### scuppernong

A light sweet table wine made from the scuppernong grape (a cultivated variety of muscadine) and named for the Scuppernong River in Tyrrel County, North Carolina.

### sherry

An amber-colored fortified wine, named for the city of Jerez de la Frontera, Spain, near which it originated. (Jerez was originally pronounced *share-us*.)

### tantalus

A locked case for wines or spirits, usually glass, named for the mythical king of Phrygia (see *tantalize*), presumably because one can see the contents but not get at them.

### tom and jerry

A hot spiced drink of rum, water, and a beaten egg, named for the fictional Tom and Jerry Hawthorne, principal characters in Pierce Egan's novel *Life in London* (1821).

## CUPS THAT CHEER . . .

### bohea

Black tea of China, named for the area where it is grown, the Wu-i Shan hills in Fukien Province. (In the Fukien dialect, Wui-i is pronounced "bui-i.") Bohea, considered a very low grade of tea, is no longer exported.

### cambric tea

Children's very weak tea, diluted with milk, named for the linen cambric (from Cambrai, France) because it is thin and white.

## Darjeeling

A fine black tea, grown in the mountainous areas of West Bengal, India, and named for the city around which the region is centered.

Darjeeling, a hill station in the days of the British Raj, commands some of the most spectacular views in the world, including Mount Kanchenjunga and, on clear days, Mount Everest in neighboring Nepal.

## java

The world's first slang term for coffee, named for the island of Java in the Dutch East Indies (now Indonesia), where the crop was introduced by the Dutch in the late seventeenth century.

Coffee originated in Arabia and remained a closely guarded secret for many centuries. At last Dutch coffee spies managed to steal some seeds and cultivate them carefully in botanical gardens, from which they spread around Europe. It was a single coffee plant from the Jardin des Plantes in Paris, stolen by an enterprising naval officer from Martinique, that became the parent of all Latin America's famed coffee plantations.

## mocha

A flavoring agent that combines chocolate and coffee, named for the seaport in Yemen, southwestern Arabia, near which coffee was first grown and from which it was shipped.

# THE STAFF OF LIFE . . .

## biscuit Tortoni

An ice-cream dessert served in a paper cup and topped with a coating of ground almonds, named for M. Tortoni, an Italian restaurateur in eighteenth-century Paris.

## graham cracker

A dry sweet cracker made of whole-wheat flour, named for the American food reformer Sylvester Graham (1794–1851). Graham preached a number of dietary reforms, but he is chiefly remembered for his campaign against bolted (sifted) white flour. The sifting process, he maintained—quite correctly—removed the most nutritious part of the wheat.

## melba toast

Bread sliced very thin and toasted until brown, named for Australian opera singer Dame Nellie Melba (1861–1931). Peach Melba (a peach half set on vanilla ice cream and covered with raspberry sauce) is also named for Dame Nellie.

Born Helen Porter Mitchell, this international operatic diva took the name "Melba" in honor of her native Melbourne.

## Parker House roll

A yeast-raised roll made by folding a circle of dough in half, named for the Parker House, famous Boston hotel, where it originated.

## Sally Lunn

A sweetened muffin, named for a female baker who sold them in the streets of Bath, England.

Some authorities dispute this origin of the name, however, and claim that it is really a corruption of *Soleilune* ("Sun Moon"), the term for a round, flat bun, yellow on top and white below.


# SOUPS . . .

## madrilene

A consommé flavored with tomato, named for the capital of Spain, Madrid.

## vichyssoise

A cold soup, made of potatoes, leeks, cream, and chicken broth, named for the city of Vichy, France. Vichyssoise is not a French soup, however, but an American one.

# SALADS AND THEIR DRESSINGS . . .

## caesar salad

A tossed salad whose dressing includes grated cheese and raw egg, named for Caesar's restaurant in Tijuana, Mexico, where it originated.

## macédoine

A mixture of cut-up fruits or vegetables, usually served as a salad, named for the Macedonian region of Greece—perhaps because a mixture of many ethnic groups is found there.

## mayonnaise

A salad dressing made of raw egg and salad oil, named for Port Mahon on the Spanish island of Minorca—probably in honor of its capture by the duke of Richelieu in 1756.

## Roquefort dressing

A dressing made with cheese from Roquefort-sur-Soulzon, France, for which it is named. (See *Roquefort cheese.*)

## Russian dressing

Mayonnaise flavored with chili sauce or catsup and pickle relish, named Russian because one of its original ingredients was caviar.

## Thousand Island dressing

Russian dressing to which are added olives and cream, named by the chef who invented it for the New York–Ontario region where the St. Lawrence River is dotted with 1,500 small islands.

## Waldorf salad

Salad of cut-up apples, celery, and nuts topped with mayonnaise, named for the Waldorf-Astoria Hotel in New York City.

# METHODS OF PREPARATION OR SERVING . . .

## lyonnaise

Prepared and seasoned with onions and parsley, named for Lyon, a city in central France known for its devotion to good food.

## Milanaise

A dish served with spaghetti, Parmesan cheese, and a tomato sauce made with truffles and mushrooms, named for the largest city in the north of Italy.

## parmentier

An adjective meaning "served with potatoes," named for the eighteenth-century French horticulturist Antoine Parmentier, who strongly advocated the cultivation and eating of potatoes.

# ENTREES . . .

## boeuf bourguignon

Beef stew garnished with onions and mushrooms, named for the wine in which it is braised, Burgundy.

## beef stroganoff

Thinly sliced beef, cooked in a sour-cream sauce and served over noodles, named for Count Paul Stroganoff, a nineteenth-century Russian diplomat.

## chateaubriand

A steak in which a pocket is cut and stuffed with seasonings before cooking, named for French writer and statesman Vicomte François René de Chateaubriand (1768–1848).

## chicken Marengo

Chicken cooked in a sauce of tomatoes, olive oil, wine, and mushrooms, named for the battlefield near Alessandria, in the Italian Piedmont, where Napoleon defeated the Austrians on June 14, 1800.

## Delmonico steak

A club steak, named for famed New York restaurateur Lorenzo Delmonico, in whose establishment it was served.

Delmonico (1813–1881), a Swiss-born American, took over his uncles' restaurant in 1832 and introduced New Yorkers to such European delicacies as eggplant, endive, and salads, and virtually created the elegant-restaurant business in this country.

## Salisbury steak

Ground beef mixed with bread crumbs, egg, milk, and seasonings, and cooked, named for English physician James J. Salisbury, a nineteenth-century food reformer. Dr. Salisbury urged his patients to eat well-done beef three times a day, along with hot water.

## Tartare steak

Ground beef mixed with egg, seasonings, and chopped onion and served raw, named for Genghis Khan's wild Tartars, who were considered capable of eating their meat uncooked.

## Wiener schnitzel ("Vienna cutlet")

Thin breaded veal cutlet, named for the Austrian capital.

# LUNCHEON MEATS . . .

## bologna

A sausage made of chopped veal, pork, and beef, then boiled and smoked, named for the city of Bologna, Italy.

## Braunschweiger

Smoked liver sausage, named for the region of Germany where it originated, Brunswick.

## frankfurter

A beef-and-pork sausage, packed in links and smoked, named for Frankfurt-am-Main, West Germany, from which came the original *Frankfurterwürstchen.*

In 1867, Charles Feltman, an itinerant pie seller, invaded Coney Island, New York, with a specially built cooking wagon, a pile of rolls, and a supply of frankfurters—and the immortal hot dog was born.

## hamburger

Ground beef, usually cooked in a flattened patty, named for the city of Hamburg, West Germany. Immigrants using the Hamburg-America shipping line were fed salt beef, taken on board at Hamburg in large pieces but chopped fine before cooking.

Today the hamburger is the basis for a massive industry that annually sells billions of these special sandwiches.

# FROM THE SEA . . .

## Bismarck herring

Herring marinated in wine, vinegar, and spices and served cold with raw onion, named for Prince Otto Edward Leopold von Bismarck (1815–1898), the Iron Chancellor of Germany and creator of the Second Reich.

## jacopever

A large-eyed reddish food fish of southern Africa, named for Jacob Evertson, a Dutch sea captain with bulging eyes and a red face.

## Little Neck clams

Young of the quahog clam when big enough to be eaten, named for Little Neck Bay, off Fort Totten, Queens, New York. Pollution of the waters caused authorities to condemn the clam beds in 1909. Nowadays, clams labeled "Little Neck" are probably drawn from other areas in and around Long Island.

## lobster Newburg

Lobster served in a sauce of sherry, egg yolk, and cream, named for a Mr. Wenburg, whose name has gotten corrupted over the years.

## lobster Thermidor

A creamy mixture of lobster, sherry, egg, and mushroom, baked in a lobster shell, named for the month of the French revolutionary calendar that corresponds roughly to July.

## sardine

A small fish of the herring family, named for the Italian island of Sardinia. The English call sardines pilchards.

# STEWS AND EGG DISHES . . .

## Brunswick stew

A stew made from two or more different meats cooked with vegetables, named for Brunswick County, Virginia, where it was originally a squirrel stew.

## Mulligan stew

A stew of whatever fish, meat, or vegetables are available, named for some unidentified Irishman.

## eggs benedict

Poached eggs and broiled ham placed on an English muffin and topped with Hollandaise sauce, named for American banker E.C. Benedict (1834–1920), who invented the dish.

## Scotch woodcock

Not a bird at all but anchovy paste on toast topped with scrambled eggs, named for a people famed for thrift.

### Yorkshire pudding

Mixture of eggs with butter, milk, and flour, baked in the drippings of roast beef, named for the largest county in England.

# SNACKS . . .

### sandwich

Filling of some kind between two slices of bread, named for John Montagu (1718–1792), the fourth earl of Sandwich. Sandwich, a confirmed gambler, was often so intent on remaining at the gaming tables that he had his servants bring his food to him there—meat between two slices of bread.

The earl served as First Lord of the Admiralty from 1771 to 1782, during which time his corrupt practices earned him the derisive nickname Jemmy Twitcher. The Hawaiian archipelago was also named in his honor by Captain James Cook: the Sandwich Islands.

### Dagwood sandwich

A combination sandwich composed of many levels of filling—meat, sausage, cheese, tomato, lettuce, etc.—named for the character Dagwood Bumstead in the comic strip *Blondie*, who habitually treats himself to such a snack, usually in the middle of the night.

# SAUCES . . .

### béarnaise

Hollandaise sauce seasoned with shallots, chervil, and tarragon, named for the ancient region of Béarn in southwestern France, now chiefly the department of Basses-Pyreñeés.

## béchamel

White sauce, sometimes enriched by cream and/or seasonings, named for Louis de Béchamel, steward to Louis XIV, who invented it.

## Bordelaise

Brown sauce (gravy made with vegetable water) flavored with Bordeaux wine, named for the Bordeaux region.

## hollandaise

Sauce made with butter, egg yolk, and either lemon juice or vinegar, served over vegetables and seafood, named for the Netherlands.

## Mornay

White sauce with cheese added, named for Philippe de Mornay (1549–1623), French Huguenot leader. A confidante to the king of Navarre (later Henry IV of France), he was known as the Huguenot Pope.

## Tabasco sauce

Trademark for a very hot sauce, used by the drop to add flavoring to other dishes, named for the Mexican state of Tabasco where it is made.

## tartar sauce

Mayonnaise flavored with pickle relish, olives, and seasoning, usually served with fish, named for Genghis Khan's Tartar hordes.

## Worcestershire sauce

Meat sauce made of soy, vinegar, anchovy, shallots, and other ingredients by the Lea & Perrins Company and named for the county in

England where it originated. Like Tabasco, Worcestershire is often a piquant ingredient in other dishes.

# VEGETABLES . . .

## Bibb lettuce

A small, tender, dark-green variety of lettuce, named for the Kentuckian who developed it, Jack Bibb.

## lima bean

A large, flat edible bean, native to tropical America and named for the capital of Peru, one of the earliest sites where Europeans settled in the New World.

Limas now form a principal ingredient in that North American favorite, succotash.

## Romaine lettuce

A long-leafed lettuce with a pronounced midrib, named the French form of "Roman" because it is a Mediterranean variety. It is also sometimes called Cos lettuce, after the Greek island of Cos.

## scallion

Green (young) onion, pulled before the bulb has had a chance to develop and usually eaten raw, named for the ancient seaport of Ascalon (now Ashkelon, Israel) from which it was shipped. Shallot, a close relative of the onion, is also named for Ascalon.

# DESSERTS . . .

## baked Alaska

Cake covered with ice-cream and meringue topping, quickly browned in an oven, named for the forty-ninth state.

## charlotte russe

Charlotte (a mold lined with lady fingers or sponge cake and covered with flavored filling of some kind) topped with whipped cream, named for the French form of "Russian."

## frangipani

Dessert of almond cream, flavored with frangipani or jasmine perfume, named for Marquis Muzio Frangipani, sixteenth-century Italian nobleman. The marquis concocted a perfume that effectively imitated the scent of the red jasmine.

## madeleine

A small rich tea cake, baked in a shell-shaped pan, named for Madeleine Paulmier, nineteenth-century French pastry cook.

## napoleon

Layers of flaky puff paste filled with cream custard and frosted on top, named for the great French soldier and politician. It is also called *mille-feuilles* ("thousand leaves") from the leafy look of the pastry when properly made.

## Nesselrode pie

Cream pie filled with flakes of preserved fruit and topped with shaved semisweet chocolate, named for Count Karl Robert von Nesselrode (1780–1862), whose chef invented it. Nesselrode, a Russian diplomat, negotiated the peace treaty that ended the Crimean War.

## Sacher torte

Torte (rich cake made with bread crumbs in place of flour) filled with apricot jam and frosted with chocolate, named for the Sacher family, Austrian hotel keepers, whose restaurant invented this famous dessert.

## Turkish delight

A jellylike confection, cut in cubes and dusted with powdered sugar, named for the Turks because it is of Near Eastern origin.

# CHEESE . . .

## Brie

A soft perishable cheese made from cow's milk, named for the region east of Paris, centered on the Marne River, where it originated.

## Caerphilly

A semisoft white cheese, named for the village in Monmouthshire, Wales, where it originated.

## Camembert

A soft cheese, whose characteristic flavor is developed by the blue mold spread over the curd during the ripening process, named for the town in Normandy where it was first made.

## cheddar

A hard yellow cheese, named for the village in Somersetshire, England, where it was invented in the seventeenth century.

The so-called American cheese is a variety of cheddar, as is nearly 80 percent of the cheeses produced in the United States.

## Cheshire

A hard cheese, similar to cheddar except that it comes in three varieties (red, blue-veined, and white), named for the English county where it originated.

One of the most famous old inns of London is the Cheshire Cheese, renowned for being the habitual resort of lexicographer Samuel Johnson.

## Creole

Unripened cheese made of cottage cheese and cream, named Creole because it originated in Louisiana.

*Creole* originally meant someone born in the New World of European parentage (an Alaska-born Russian, for example), but in Louisiana the word has come to mean a person of mixed Negro, Spanish, and French ancestry and the colorful local culture these people have developed.

## Edam

A semifirm Dutch cheese, molded in cannonball form and covered with a thin wax rind, named for the town north of Amsterdam where it is made.

## Gorgonzola

Italian blue cheese, made of cow's milk, flavored with fungus from local caves, named for the village near Milan where it was originally made.

## Gouda

A rich semifirm cheese, made in round or loaf-shaped molds and named for the town between the Hague and Utrecht, the Netherlands, where it is made.

## Herkimer

A sharp variety of cheddar, molded in large wheels, named for Herkimer County, New York, where it is made.

## Liederkranz ("Song Circle")

A soft pungent cheese of American origin, named for a German-American singing society in New York City. Emil Frey, a delicatessen owner, created this strong-smelling cheese in 1850 and named it for the Liederkranz Club (still in existence) to which he belonged.

## Limburger

A semisoft cheese of strong flavor and even stronger smell, named for the Belgian city of Limburg where it was developed.

## Monterey Jack

A jack cheese (a semisoft white cheese normally of high moisture content) that is atypically dry, named for Monterey County, California, where it originated.

## Münster

A mild-flavored soft cheese, named for the city of Münster in ancient Alsace (now Haut-Rhin), France.

## Parmesan

A hard, dry cheese, used chiefly for grating and garnishing other dishes, named for Parma, Italy, from which it comes.


## Roquefort

The blue cheese par excellence, made from sheep's milk and ripened in caves, named for the town where it originated, Roquefort-sur-Soulzon, department of Aveyron, south-central France.


## Stilton

A blue-veined cheese with a wrinkled crust, named for the village in Huntingdonshire, England, where it was first popularized.

In the early eighteenth century, the Bell Inn at Stilton was a regular coach stop on the North Road between London and Glasgow, and when the cheese was served to passengers, it so delighted them that they carried word of it all over England. Today connoisseurs regard it as England's finest cheese.


## Swiss cheese

A hard, pale, big-holed cheese, named (in America) for its country of origin. In Switzerland itself, this cheese is called Emmentaler (from the valley where it originated as long ago as the fifteenth century), and in France and England, Gruyère, after the town in the canton of Fribourg.

Swiss cheese is considered one of the most difficult varieties to produce by natural means, for three different strains of bacteria are needed to obtain the proper form of fermentation. However, modern methods introduce the bacteria artificially and thus reduce the chance of failing. The finished product is turned out in massive wheels, sometimes six inches thick and four feet in diameter, weighing up to 220 pounds.


## Tilsiter

A sharp-flavored, semifirm cheese, named for Tilsit, East Prussia (now Sovetsk, Soviet Union), where it originated.

# FRUIT . . .

### Bartlett pear

A plump yellow pear, called *bon Chrétien* ("good Christian") in England and France, named for the American merchant who first marketed them in this country.

Enoch Bartlett (1779–1860) bought a farm in Roxbury, Massachusetts, from one Thomas Brewer, and found several trees of these pears growing there. He sold them as Bartlett pears, and they have carried the name ever since.

### Boysenberry

A hybrid berry, developed from the loganberry and several varieties of raspberry and blackberry, named for the American horticulturist who bred them, Rudolph Boysen.

### cantaloupe

A muskmelon with a warty rind and a sweet orange flesh, named for the Italian papal villa where it was first cultivated, Cantalupo.

### damson

A small, dark-purple plum, named for Damascus, capital of Syria, because it is of Asia Minor origin.

### greengage

A sweet green plum imported into England from France by, and named for, Sir William Gage (1777–1864), a botanist.

## Jonathan

An apple developed in the Hudson Valley, New York State, early in the nineteenth century and named for an American jurist, Jonathan Hasbrouck.

## loganberry

A wine-red, tart, flavorful berry, thought to be a natural hybrid between the wild blackberry and the red raspberry, first grown and named for Judge James H. Logan (1841–1928) in Santa Cruz County, California.

## mandarin orange

Reddish-orange, loose-skinned fruit, whose tree is native to China, named probably because its color is similar to that of a mandarin's robe. (Mandarins were government officials in Imperial China.) The tangerine was developed from the mandarin orange by hybridization.

## McIntosh

A tangy green-red eating apple, named for John McIntosh, who discovered the fruit tree growing wild on his farm in Ontario, Canada, about 1811. "Mack's" are still favorites with both Canadians and Americans.

## Natal plum

An edible scarlet fruit resembling a true plum, native to southern Africa, named for Natal Province, Union of South Africa.

Vasco da Gama, Portuguese explorer, sighted this part of Africa on December 25, 1497, and hence named it Terra Natalis—"land of the Nativity."

## peach

A succulent fruit of the plum family, whose name is a corruption of *Persicus* ("Persian"). Peaches are native to China, but they arrived in Europe by way of the Near East and hence were thought of as Persian fruit.

## Saint-John's-Bread

Fruit of the carob, a tree of the Mediterranean region, named for John the Baptist, because its locustlike pods provide food for both animals and men. The reference is probably to John's stay in the wilderness:

And John was clothed with camel's hair, and with a girdle of a skin about his loins; and he did eat locusts and wild honey. (Mark 1:6)

In ancient times carob seeds were used as weight standards. The word "carat," a weight unit for precious stones, is derived from carob.

## tangerine

A cultivated form of hybrid mandarin orange, named for the Moroccan seaport of Tangier, from which it was exported.

# AND NUTS . . .

## Bertholetta

A genus of tall South American trees, named for Comte Claude Louis Berthollet (1748–1822), French chemist. The Bertholetta yields a large fruit containing several hard-shelled triangular seeds known as Brazil nuts.

### filbert

A sweet-flavored nut, also called the hazelnut, named for Saint Philibert (d. 684), French abbot, whose feast day, August 20, falls in the nutting season.

### macadamia nut

Hard-shelled nut similar to a filbert, fruit of the macadamia tree, named for John Macadam, Australian chemist. The evergreen macadamia is native to Australia.

### walnut

An edible nut produced by a tree of the genus Juglans, whose name is a corruption of *Welsh nut*. In medieval times, to the English "Welshman" was synonymous with "foreigner," and it was known that these nut trees were not native to England.

What we call the English walnut is known elsewhere as the Persian walnut, the French walnut, and the Circassian walnut. Its actual land of origin is uncertain, but it is thought to be either China or the Himalayas.

The native American black walnut, a closely related species, yields an edible nut also, but its chief use is as a flavoring agent in ice cream and candy. The wood of this same tree is one of the most desirable of furniture woods.

## AFTER-DINNER TOBACCO . . .

### Havana

Probably the world's finest cigar, named for the capital of Cuba, where cigars were rolled.

The Spanish colonies long held a monopoly of the trade in smoking tobacco, because the species native to the tropics, *Nicotiana tabacum*, was naturally more mellow and smokable than the harsh variety found in the northern colonies, *Nicotiana rustica*. Then in 1611, an early

Virginia settler obtained some of the precious Spanish seeds and tried them out at Jamestown, and the monopoly was broken.

Nevertheless, the Spanish colonies continued to produce tobacco of a superior grade, and from this crop the trade in fine Havana cigars developed.

## maccaboy

A perfumed snuff named for the town at the northern tip of Martinique, where it was produced.

## oronoco

A variety of tobacco, grown in North America but named for the region from which it supposedly originated, the Orinoco River, Venezuela. Oronoco is thought to be the plant from which modern bright leaves and burleys (cigarette tobaccos) were developed.

## perique

A tough-fibered, strong-flavored tobacco, raised in St. James Parish, Louisiana (a few miles west of New Orleans in the bayou country), and named for planter Pierre Chenet. Chenet, whose nickname was Périque, developed and introduced the variety, which is used chiefly in mixtures.

## stogy

A cheap, slender cigar, whose name is short for *Conestoga cigar*. Stogies were a favorite smoke with the men who drove the Conestoga wagons—huge, boat-shaped freight wagons manufactured in Conestoga, Pennsylvania. (See *Conestoga wagons*.)

# · 7 ·

# Clothing:
# A Complete Wardrobe

With the advent of the fourth glacial period, some 25,000 years ago, the people of the world were no longer able to migrate to warmer climates. Thus began humankind's need for body covering.

At first this necessity of life was satisfied by furs or skins crudely wrapped around the body. But, as society progressed, the art of weaving was invented, and soon men and women were dressing themselves as much for show as for warmth. Style and fashion were quick to follow, and with them the distinctions of rank and wealth expressed in clothing.

## SHOES . . .

Shoes have often meant more than mere protection of the feet. In many cultures the kind of shoes one wore symbolized one's rank or prestige. The poor wore nothing.

In Egypt, only important individuals wore *sandals*, a shoe that can be traced back four thousand years and which was probably named for the Lydian god Sandal. The ancient Greeks took their sandals off before they entered their houses. The Romans wore their sandals indoors but forbade slaves to do the same. The Roman aristocracy distinguished themselves by wearing sandals with a moon-shaped design on the backs.

Greek warriors went to battle wearing one sandal, on their left feet, as protection and to kick opponents in the groin.

Sandals in India signified regal power.

Religiously, ancient Semitic peoples helped consummate the vows of newlyweds by throwing shoes at them or tying them to their persons. Muslims, Hindus, and other religious groups take their shoes off before entering places of worship.

## alaska

An overshoe with a sole of rubber and uppers of rubberized cloth, named for the forty-ninth state.

## Argyle socks

Socks made with a tartanlike knitting pattern, named for the Campbells of Argyll (a county in western Scotland), from whose clan tartan the sock design was supposedly adapted.

The name is spelled two different ways, but the above are the preferred forms for socks and county, respectively.

## balmoral

A variety of oxford, named for Balmoral Castle, Aberdeenshire, Scotland, summer home of British sovereigns.

## bluchers

Another variety of oxford, named for Field Marshal Gebhard Leberecht von Blücher (1742–1819), the tough old Prussian soldier who helped Wellington defeat Napoleon at Waterloo, June 18, 1815. He was seventy-three at the time.

## Congress gaiters

A high shoe with elastic gussets at the sides, named for the U.S. Congress, since it was popular with members.

## Cuban heel

A broad, medium-high, straight-lined heel, named for the largest island in the Caribbean.

## French heel

A high woman's heel, set well forward and forming in profile a pronounced curve, named for the fashion-conscious French.

## Hessians

A man's knee-length boot whose top is higher at the front than at the back, named for the people of Hesse, West Germany, who popularized it around 1800.

## juliet

A woman's slipper with high front and back and low sides, similar to a man's slipper called a romeo, named for the principal characters in Shakespeare's tragic romance, *Romeo and Juliet*.

## oxford

A low shoe laced up the front (three or more pairs of eyelets), the common shoe of the twentieth century, named for the industrial and academic city of Oxford, England.

## Spanish heel

A very high woman's heel, wood covered with leather, whose profile is curved at the heel end and straight at the arch end, named for Spain, perhaps because heel-clicking is typical of Spanish dance forms.

## wellingtons

Knee-length boot with loose-fitting top higher in front than at the back, named for Arthur Wellesley, duke of Wellington (1769–1852), the Iron Duke who presided over the final defeat of Napoleon at Waterloo in 1815.

# UNDERGARMENTS . . .

## balbriggans

Underwear and/or pajamas made of a knitted cotton fabric named for the town of Balbriggan, County Dublin, Ireland, where it was manufactured.

## bloomers

Loose underpants gathered (usually with elastic) around the waist and at the leg ends, named for Mrs. Amelia Jenks Bloomer (1818–1894), early social reformer.

Mrs. Bloomer, an ardent supporter of women's rights, advocated dress reform on the grounds that the vast hoop skirts of her day were immodest, expensive, difficult to manage, and dangerous (easily caught in machinery when women worked in factories). She herself appeared publicly in a costume consisting of a knee-length dress over a pair of Turkish trousers gathered at the ankle. Since then, "bloomers" has come to mean any leg-covering that is full enough to need gathering at top and bottom.

# TROUSERS . . .

## denim

A durable twilled cotton fabric, used for making work and sports clothes, named for the city where it was originally manufactured, Nimes, Gard, France. It was known then as *serge de Nimes*, which soon became shortened to "denim."

## jeans

A twilled cotton cloth, similar to denim and also used for making work clothes, named for the French form of Genoa, where it was manufactured—Gênes.

## jodhpurs

Riding breeches cut loose across the hips, close-fitting from knee to ankle, with a strap that goes under the boot, named for Jodhpur, Rajasthan, India, where native princes wore similar garments.

## knickers

Rather loosely fitting breeches gathered just below the knee, named for Diedrich Knickerbocker, the fictitious author of Washington Irving's *History of New York*.

"Father Knickerbocker" is still the personification of New York City, just as "Uncle Sam" is of the United States.

## leotard

Tights, sometimes attached to a closely fitting garment covering the torso and arms, named for Jules Léotard, nineteenth-century French trapeze artist. Monsieur Léotard, who perfected the aerial somersault, once said of his performing costume, "Do you want to be adored by the ladies? . . . Put on a more natural garb, which does not hide your best features."

## Levi's

Trade name for work pants of denim, reinforced at the pocket with rivets, named for San Francisco manufacturer Levi Strauss.

Strauss, an impoverished immigrant tailor, arrived in San Francisco with nothing but a bolt of canvas, which he hoped to make into tents to sell in the gold-mining camps. The cloth turned out to be too lightweight for tents, so when a miner complained to him that he couldn't buy work pants that would last, Strauss used it to tailor a pair of trousers.

That first pair made such a solid hit that other miners were soon clamoring for similar garments, and Strauss was in business. When the canvas ran out, he imported some *serge de Nimes* (see *denim*) and used that instead. Later, some nameless miner, tired of pockets popping open from the ore samples stuck in them, had a local blacksmith rivet the corners in place, and that's how America's best-known work garment came into being. Called variously dungarees, blue jeans, or Levi's, they are in demand literally around the world.

### pants

A short term for "pantaloons," close-fitting trousers with straps that pass under the foot (like Uncle Sam's), named for the character Pantaloon in the Commedia dell' Arte, a foolish old man who wears slippers and tight-fitting leg coverings.

The character probably took his name from Saint Pantaleon, a fourth-century Christian physician reputedly martyred by Diocletian.

### Sam Browne belt

A leather waist belt with a strap that crosses over the right shoulder, worn by officers in the British and American armies, named for Sir Samuel James Browne (1824–1901), a one-armed British general.

The belt was originally a sword belt, but by World War I it supported only an officer's side arms. Since it distinguished an officer from common soldiers, it provided a sharp-sighted enemy a specific target to aim for, and many American officers, at any rate, soon ceased to wear it at the battlefront.

# SHIRTS AND SWEATERS . . .

### cardigan

A collarless sweater that buttons down the front, named for Lieutenant Colonel James Thomas Brudenell, seventh Earl of Cardigan

(1797–1868), who often wore a knitted woolen waistcoat while commanding the Light Brigade of Cavalry during the Crimean War.

Stupid, irascible, blindly courageous, Cardigan led his men in the famous charge of the Light Brigade at Balaclava, October 25, 1854—a mile and a half up a narrow valley lined with enemy artillery—and was one of the few who came out alive.

### garibaldi

A woman's shirtwaist, modeled after the red shirt worn by nineteenth-century followers of Italian patriot Giuseppi Garibaldi and named for him. The garibaldi was a tailored shirt of red cloth with long sleeves, a small turned-down collar, and a fly-front neck opening with four buttons.

### guernsey

A sailor's knitted woolen shirt, named for the island of Guernsey in the Channel Island, where many of the men are seamen.

### jersey

A pullover shirt of knitted cotton fabric, named for the Channel Island of Jersey. Knitted fabrics are thought to have been invented in the Channel Islands in the fifteenth century, when it was found that a knitted tunic absorbed sea spray but did not feel wet, and hence was the most comfortable garment for a sailor or fisherman to take to sea.

# COLLARS AND TIES . . .

### ascot

A broad double-knot neckcloth whose square ends are doubled over and held in place by a stickpin, named for the fashionable racecourse near the village of Ascot, Berkshire, England. Ascots are worn with a cutaway coat and (usually) a gray top hat, especially for the four-day Royal Meeting in June and the running of the Gold Cup.

## Bertha collar

A wide round collar covering the shoulders and sometimes the throat, often made of lace or crochet work, named for Berthe, queen of the Franks (d. 783), the mother of Charlemagne. Queen Berthe was famed for her modesty.

## cravat

A broad linen neckcloth, wrapped twice around the neck and then tied in a knot, named for Cravate, the French form of Croatia. In 1660, a Croatian regiment appeared in Paris, sporting colorful knotted neckerchiefs, and the name caught on. However, cravats themselves did not become popular until the French Revolution, when they became part of the accepted revolutionists' garb.

## Eton collar

A wide flat collar turned down over the lapels of the jacket, named for Eton College, Buckinghamshire, England, where it is worn as part of the school's traditional costume.

## Napoleon collar

A high-standing coat collar worn with a black satin cravat, named for the Emperor Napoleon, whose uniforms were made with collars of this kind.

## Peter Pan collar

A round collar with rounded ends, named for the fictional hero of Sir James Barrie's play *Peter Pan*.

## Vandyke collar

A falling band, a broad collar of fine lawn edged with lace, named for portraitist Anthony Van Dyke because so many of his sitters wore such collars.

## Windsor tie

A loosely knotted tie, knot fatter than the usual four-in-hand knot, named for the duke of Windsor, who popularized the style in the 1930's when he was Prince of Wales.

# SUITS—OF SORTS . . .

## bikini

A scanty two-piece bathing suit for women, named for the atoll in the Marshall Islands, Micronesia, where the United States conducted atom bomb tests in the late 1940's.

## tuxedo

A single- or double-breasted dinner jacket, usually black for winter and white for summer, named for the fashionable resort community of Tuxedo Park, New York, where it was first worn and popularized.

# OVERCOATS . . .

## balmacaan

A loose, flaring coat with raglan sleeves, usually of raincoat fabric, named for Balmacaan, an estate near Inverness, Scotland.

# British warm

A short heavy coat fastened with rope loops and wooden toggles, worn for outdoor sports in winter and named British because it was first popularized there. Shortly after World War II, the Royal Navy made its surplus pea jackets available to civilians, and these evolved into the British warm, popular especially among skiers.

# chesterfield

A single-breasted, knee-length overcoat with a velvet collar and flap pockets, named for a turn-of-the-century earl of Chesterfield.

# Eisenhower jacket

A waist-length belted military jacket in olive-drab, usually with a zippered front, named for General of the Army Dwight David Eisenhower (1890–1969), American commander-in-chief in Europe during World War II, who favored such an informal garment on active duty.

# joseph

An eighteenth-century ladies' redingote, or riding coat, with caped shoulders, fitted waist, floor-length skirt, and buttons down the front, named for the biblical Joseph, known for his coat of many colors.

# Macfarlane coat

A topcoat with capes in place of sleeves, invented in the 1850's and named for some unknown Mr. Macfarlane.

# mackinaw

An outdoorsman's jacket of blanket material, often bright plaid, belted at the waist, named for Mackinaw City, Michigan, near the site of Fort Michilimackinac, an important early trading post.

## Mackintosh

A raincoat, originally of rubberized cotton, named for Charles Mackintosh (1766–1843), Scots chemist, who patented the first successful waterproofing process and designed the first coat manufactured of waterproof fabric.

## palatine

A short cape, covering the neck and shoulders, named for Elizabeth Charlotte of Bavaria, Princess Palatine (d. 1722), sister-in-law of Louis XIV, who popularized it in the seventeenth century.

## Prince Albert

A knee-length double-breasted frock coat (a coat made with bodice and skirts in separate pieces joined at the waist), less close-fitting than the usual frock coat, named for Albert Edward, Prince of Wales, who popularized the garment in the late nineteenth century.

## raglan

A loose-fitting overcoat with raglan sleeves (sleeves whose inset line runs from the underarm to the neck), named for Field Marshal Fitzroy James Henry Somerset, Lord Raglan (1788–1855), commander-in-chief of British forces during the Crimean War.

## roquelaure

A knee-length woolen cloak, popular throughout the eighteenth century in both Europe and America, named for Antoine Gaston Jean Baptiste, duke of Roquelaure (1656–1738).

## spencer

A short, closely fitted jacket worn by both men and women, named for George John, second earl of Spencer (1758–1834). Spencer claimed that fashion was so essentially absurd that he could invent a style himself and proved it by cutting the tails off his coat and strolling about London in what was left of the garment. Within a few weeks, the spencer was all the rage.

Spencer served as Pitt's First Lord of the Admiralty and as such was the man who named Lord Nelson to command in the Mediterranean, an appointment that eventually led to the Battle of Trafalgar.

### ulster

A long, boxy, double-breasted overcoat, usually with a belt in the back, named for the province of Ulster, Northern Ireland, because it was originally made of Ulster frieze (a heavy woolen cloth manufactured in Ireland).

## GOWNS AND DRESSES . . .

### Basque bodice

A form-fitting bodice with a short, skirtlike extension at the bottom, worn over a bustle, named for the people of the Pyrenees, who were so often fishermen. In the 1870's, Alexandra, Princess of Wales, inadvertently set the style for Basque bodices by appearing for a fishing expedition wearing a fisherman's jersey over her gown.

### Dolly Varden

A woman's style of dress, fashionable in the 1870's, which consisted of a polonaise with bustle of printed cretonne over an underskirt of some bright color, set off with a flowered hat, named for the fictional Dolly Varden in Charles Dickens' *Barnaby Rudge*. The flirtatious Dolly was characterized by love of colorful clothes.

### Mameluke sleeve

A long sleeve consisting of a series of puffs, tied with ribbons, from shoulder to wrist, named for the Mamelukes (the warlike descendants of

Christian slaves in Egypt) recruited into the French army by Napoleon.

Worn by men and women both in the sixteenth and seventeenth centuries (then called a virago sleeve), this style staged a brief comeback in women's clothes during the Empire.

## mantua

An eighteenth-century woman's robe or gown, worn open down the front to display elegant underbodice and skirt, named for the town of Mantua, Lombardy, Italy, since it was often made of Mantua silk.

A mantua-maker was a dressmaker, later a cloak maker (probably through the confusion of "mantua" with "mantle"). Until late in the seventeenth century, all women's garments, like men's, were made by tailors. But then the two trades began to split off, and women were soon obtaining their wardrobes from couturiers (dressmakers), mantua-makers (cloak makers), and modistes (milliners).

## Mother Hubbard

A long loose gown, hanging from a yoke, named after the nursery-rhyme character.

## polonaise

A tight-fitting bodice attached to an elaborately draped overskirt, worn over a matching underskirt, named for the French form of "Polish." The polonaise, popular at the French court at the time of the American Revolution, was often worn with a short (ankle-length) skirt to form a "shepherdess" outfit, when Marie Antoinette and her ladies played at being "just folks."

# HEADGEAR . . .

## balaclava

A hoodlike knitted cap, closely covering head, throat (and sometimes chin), and part of the shoulders, named for the village of Balaklava near

Sevastopol, Soviet Union, where it was first worn during the Crimean War. Today balaclavas are often worn by soldiers, mountaineers, or explorers for warmth under other headgear.

## balmoral

The traditional blue bonnet of Scotland, a flat beret, named for Balmoral Castle, Aberdeenshire, Scotland. Worn for centuries by gentleman and commoner, soldier and civilian alike, the balmoral is woven in one piece without a seam and sports a red or blue pompom on top plus, usually, a cockade, a feather, or sprig of greenery as a clan badge.

## bangkok

A hoodlike hat woven of Bangkok straw, made from fibers of a tree that grows in the vicinity of the Thai capital and named for it.

## bowler

A round, hard-topped hat of stiff felt with a curled brim, named for London hatmaker William Bowler, who designed it in 1850. Originally it was intended as a protective headpiece for a man named William Cole to wear on hunting trips, but it has come to signify (in England) the correctly garbed civil servant.

In America, where it is much less popular, the bowler is called a derby after a nineteenth-century earl of Derby who wore it to the races at Epsom Downs.

## fedora

The prevailing hat style for men, consisting of a soft felt crown with a center crease and a flexible brim, named for the title character of Victorien Sardou's play *Fédora*, which starred Sarah Bernhardt.

Ironically, the hat that is worn today exclusively by men started out as a feminine fashion. Worn with a feather and a veil, it was a favorite for cycling.

## fez

A brimless felt cap or tarboosh in the shape of a truncated cone, worn by men in North Africa and the Near East, named for the city of Fez in Morocco, where it originated. The long black tassel on top symbolizes a lock of hair that used to be worn by Muslim men, by means of which Allah pulled them to Paradise.

## Gandhi cap

A white cotton cap without brim or visor but with a wide band, worn by many people in India and popularized by the political and spiritual leader Mohandas K. Gandhi (1869–1948). It became the symbol of his political followers, the Congress Party.

## Glengarry

A woolen cap, folded in the center when not worn, edged with black ribbon that terminates in lappets hanging down the back of the neck, named for the MacDonells of Glengarry, Scotland, who were the first to wear it.

## havelock

A cap covering with an extended piece to protect the back of the neck (à la the French Foreign Legion), named for Sir Henry Havelock (1795–1857), British general famed for his concern over the well-being of his men.

Havelock distinguished himself during the Indian Mutiny of 1857, and held the besieged city of Lucknow for two months until relieved.

## Homburg

A man's hat of stiff felt made with a high creased crown and a slightly curled brim, named for the city of Homburg, West Germany, where it was manufactured. The Homburg, which has an "important" appearance, is considered the "correct" headgear for a successful businessman.

## jinnah cap

A tarboosh similar to the Near Eastern fez but made of karakul fur, named for the founder of Pakistan, Mohammed Ali Jinnah (1876–1948), who wore such a headpiece as a symbol of his Islamic religion.

## Mary Stuart cap

A close-fitting woman's cap that comes down to a point on the forehead, often decorated with a pearl drop, named for Mary Stuart, Queen of Scots (1542–1587), who wore such a cap during her widowhood. Mary was widowed three times.

Hair that is naturally shaped in a similar point on the forehead is called a widow's peak.

## Mexican sombrero

A straw hat with a relatively low conical crown and an enormously wide brim, usually curled at the edges, named for Mexico, where it originated and is chiefly worn.

## Panama hat

A hat of finely plaited straw of jipajapa leaves, worn in the tropics for its lightweight coolness and named for Panama because it was there that North Americans first encountered it. Actually it is made in Ecuador, Peru, and Colombia.

## stetson

The so-called ten-gallon cowboy hat, a high-crowned and broad-brimmed hat worn chiefly in the American Southwest, named for Philadelphia hatmaker John B. Stetson (1830–1906), who began making them in 1868.

## tam-o'-shanter

A wide floppy balmoral, usually of tartan, with a tight-fitting band and a pompom on top, named for the folk hero Tam O'Shanter, about whom Robert Burns wrote a long narrative poem.

# COIFFURES AND FACIAL HAIR . . .

Hair, intended by nature as a protection from the cold, has been turned by man into an expression of fashion and culture. Primitive men put feathers and bones in their hair to impress their enemies. In Great Britain and some other countries the wig symbolizes judges and barristers. A black lacquered wig is an essential part of a Japanese geisha's costume. In Turkestan, an unmarried girl wears her hair tied in forty little braids, but after marriage and childbearing, she wears two large braids. Among the African Masai, women and nonwarriors must shave their heads. In the Middle Ages Christian monks, priests, and friars shaved the crown of the head, so that the tonsure became the symbol of the clergy. Buddhist monks shave their whole heads, and Muslim men wear a single long tassel of hair by which Allah is to lift them to heaven.

## Afro

Stiff, curly hair shaped in a round bush, named for Afro-Americans, who popularized this style in the 1960's. It is sometimes also called a natural, since the hair is left in its natural state, unstraightened.

## Charley

Short, pointed beard, named for Charles I, King of England (1600–1649), who wore one.

## dundrearies

Flowing side whiskers combined with a separate moustache, named for the fictional character Lord Dundreary in the nineteenth-century vulgar comedy, *Our American Cousin*—famed chiefly because Lincoln was watching it the night he was assassinated.

The play's author, English playwright Tom Taylor (1817–1880), was best known for a different fictional character, Hawkshaw the Detective in *The Ticket of Leave Man*.

## marcel

A method of curling the hair in deep, regular waves, named for Marcel Grateau, nineteenth-century French hairdresser. Grateau used a curling iron to "marcel" women's hair and made his fortune at the age of twenty-three, but it was not until the 1930's that the marcel achieved its widest popularity.

## pompadour

A hair style for both men and women in which the hair is brushed up from the forehead and straight back, often over a padded roll, named for Jeanne Antoinette Poisson (1721–1764), marquise de Pompadour, mistress of Louis XV. Pompadour maintained her position as favorite for twenty years, during which time she exerted a deep and disastrous effect on French foreign policy.

## sideburns

Side whiskers, especially a continuation of the side hair down the cheeks and across the upper lip, worn with a smooth chin, named for Major General Ambrose E. Burnsides (1824–1881), American Civil War soldier who sported such whiskers. In England a similar kind of facial-hair style but without the moustache is known as muttonchop whiskers.

## Vandyke

An elegant combination of pointed chin beard and moustache, named for portraitist Anthony Van Dyke, whose sitters frequently wore this seventeenth-century style.

# JEWELRY . . .

## brummagem

An adjective often applied to paste jewelry imitating the real thing, named for Birmingham, England, where counterfeit groats (fourpence pieces) were coined in the seventeenth century.

## lavaliere

An ornamental pendant or locket hanging from a fine chain, named for Louise de la Baume le Blanc, duchesse de La Vallière (1644–1710), mistress of Louis XIV.

## pinchbeck

An alloy of copper and zinc used to imitate gold in the manufacture of cheap jewelry, named for Christopher Pinchbeck (1670–1732), a London watchmaker who invented it. "Pinchbeck" as an adjective has thus come to mean anything cheap and/or spurious.

## rhinestone

A colorless, glittery stone manufactured to imitate diamonds, named for the district in France, Bas-Rhin, where rhinestones were first made.

## Talmi gold

Gold-plated brass, named for the Parisian who created it, a Monsieur Tallois. The French called it *Tallois-demi-or* ("Tallois half gold"), which became shortened to Talmi gold.

# SCENTS . . .

## cologne

*Eau de Cologne* ("water of Cologne"), a light scent consisting of aromatic oils thinned with alcohol, named for the French form of Köln, West Germany, where it was first produced. The original *Kölnisch wasser* is better known as 4711, from the address of the firm that developed it, 4711 Glockengasse ("Bell Street").

## Florida Water

Trademark for a lightly scented after-shave lotion, named for the state of Florida possibly because orange-flower water is an important ingredient.

## neroli oil

Orange-flower oil, an essential oil used in the manufacture of perfume, named for Anna Maria de la Tremoille, princess of Nerole, Italy, who popularized its use in the seventeenth century.

# RELIGIOUS GARMENTS . . .

## dalmatic

A Mass vestment with loose sleeves, worn by deacon or subdeacon assisting the celebrant, named for Dalmatia, the coastal district along the Adriatic in Yugoslavia.

## Geneva gown and bands

A loose black academic gown, worn with a clerical collar from which depend two white lawn bands, favored especially by Calvinist clergymen and named for the city of Geneva, the home of John Calvin (1509–1564), Protestant religious reformer.

## Roman collar

A clerical collar buttoned in back, named Roman because it is most often associated with Roman Catholic clergy.

### sanbenito

A sackcloth smock worn by medieval penitents, named for the founder of medieval monasticism, Saint Benedict (San Benito) (480–547), because it resembled a monk's habit. Victims of the Inquisition wore sanbenitos on their way to the flames—yellow with a red cross if they were penitent, black painted with scenes of hell if they were not.

# FASHIONS . . .

### Beau Brummel

A male fashion plate, named for George Bryan Brummell (1778–1840), famed Regency dandy, who was nicknamed Beau (French for "handsome") for his care in dressing.

A crony of the Prince of Wales (later the Prince Regent and later still King George IV), Brummell set men's styles for the entire court and thence much of Europe. He preferred trousers to breeches and dark, well-tailored coats to the embroidered and laced garments of the eighteenth century, and his influence on men's fashions has persisted nearly to our own day.

### Grecian bend

A posture style of the 1870's, in which the upper half of a woman's body appears to be pushed forward, while the bottom half (aided by a bustle) juts out to the rear, named Grecian perhaps because in profile it was supposed to form a gracefully curved line.

### spruce

Smart, chic, dapper, named for the old English word for Prussia, because the fine leather used in jerkins and other garments came from there.

"To spruce up" means to make oneself neat and presentable.

## Watteau

An adjective describing a style of dress fashionable during the French Regency (1715–1723), named for the painter Jean Antoine Watteau (1684–1721), since so many of his subjects appear in it. A Watteau gown (or sacque) is a loose billowy garment, falling from the shoulders in back, worn over a tightly laced bodice and full underskirt, and accompanied by a Watteau bonnet, a small flat hat worn on the front of the head and elaborately decorated with ostrich plumes, lace, and narrow ribbons.

## zephyr

An adjective which, when applied to garments, means "summery, lightweight," named for the mythological Zephyrus, the Greek god of the west wind.

# CLOTHING MATERIAL . . .

## baldachin

A gold-embroidered silk fabric, used chiefly for church vestments and decorations, named for Baldacco, the Italian form of Baghdad. This ancient city (now the capital of Iraq) was renowned for its rich brocades.

## batiste

A delicate, nearly transparent fabric originally made of linen, named for Jean Baptiste de Cambrai, a thirteenth-century weaver who invented it. It is used today chiefly in women's blouses and infants' christening gowns.

## Bedford cord

A worsted fabric woven with lengthwise raised cords, named for New Bedford, Massachusetts, where it originated.

## bengaline

A fabric composed of a silk warp and woolen weft, producing a pronounced crosswise ribbed effect, named for the province of Bengal, India (now Bangladesh), where it originated.

## buckram

A coarse cotton fabric sized with glue and used for stiffening parts of garments, hats, and bookbindings, named for Bukhara, a city in Uzbek, Soviet Union, where it originated. Bukhara was once considered an Islamic holy city and was a major training center for Muslim priests.

## calico

A cheap cotton textile, printed with a design on one side, named for the city from which it was shipped, Calicut (now Kozhikode), India.

Calico is one of the oldest known of fabrics and has been woven in India for at least a thousand years. In the early eighteenth century, English textile manufacturers, fearing competition, got their government to pass the Calico Act, which prevented the importation of the Indian product for fifty years.

In America, where hot summers made a cheap, pretty, lightweight fabric extremely popular, calico has always been a favorite.

## cambric

A delicate closely woven linen fabric, named for the city where it originated, Cambrai, Nord, France, formerly part of Flanders. Cambric is so frequently used for dainty handkerchiefs that "a square of cambric" is synonymous with "handkerchief."

## chambray

A fabric of linen, cotton, or synthetics, woven with a colored warp and white weft for a frosty look, named for Cambrai, Nord, France, where it originated.

# cretonne

White cloth splashily printed with floral designs, named for the village of Creton in Normandy, France. Cretonne is chiefly used in summer slipcovers and draperies.

# damask

A linen or cotton fabric with a pattern woven in, named for Damascus, Syria, where it was first produced. The pattern appears on one side shiny against dull and on the other dull against shiny. Damask is most commonly used for fine table linens.

# dotted Swiss

A sheer cotton fabric ornamented with regularly spaced dots, named for its country of origin. Dotted Swiss is, in fact, still manufactured in Switzerland. It is used for children's summer frocks and for curtains.

# galatea

A striped cotton twill, used for informal shoes, beach clothes, and sportswear, named for H.M.S. *Galatea*, a British man-of-war. Galatea was first used particularly in children's sailor suits.

# georgette

A silk or silk-mixture fabric, named for Madame Georgette de la Plante of Paris, a noted couturier.

# holland

A stout linen cloth, usually unbleached, named for the Netherlands, where it was made. Originally used for drawers and other undergarments, holland cloth is now usually heavily stiffened and made into window shades.

## jaconet

A soft white linen fabric slightly heavier than cambric, named for Jagannath, India, where it was originally made. Jaconet is used chiefly in infants' wear and, when waterproofed, for bandages.

## Kendal green

A kind of woolen cloth, typically green in color, named for the town of Kendal in Westmoreland, England.

## linsey-woolsey

A sturdy fabric woven with a warp of cotton and weft of wool, named for the village of Lindsey in Suffolk, England, where it originated.

Linsey-woolsey was a popular fabric in the American colonies, especially on the frontier. Backwoodsmen might wear leggings of fringed buckskin, but they preferred their hunting shirts of linsey-woolsey.

## lisle

A fine cotton thread used in the manufacture of underwear, gloves, and hosiery, named for Lisle (now Lille), Nord, France, where it was first manufactured. The smooth finish of this long-staple cotton thread is obtained by passing it over jet flames to remove the fuzz.

## madras

A fine cotton shirt fabric with pattern (stripes or checks) woven in like gingham, named for the port of Madras, India. A variety of this textile, called bleeding madras, runs when laundered, creating an interesting color effect.

## melton

A heavy felted woolen fabric, used in the manufacture of overcoats and military uniforms, named for Melton Mowbray in Leicestershire, England, where it is woven.

## mercerized

An adjective meaning "treated with caustic soda," named for John Mercer (1791–1866), English calico printer and chemist, who developed the process. Cotton fabrics and sewing thread are mercerized to make them glossier, stronger, and more receptive to dyes.

## muslin

A plain-woven cotton fabric, named for the city of Mosul, Iraq, where it was originally manufactured. Muslin comprises weaves as sheer as batiste and as heavy as industrial cloth, but it is best known as sheet and pillowcase material.

## organdy

A sheer muslin, slightly stiff, named for the ancient city of Urgandy (now Urgench), Uzbek, Soviet Union, where it originated. Because of its diaphanous quality, organdy is a popular fabric for bridal and evening wear.

## orphrey

A richly detailed piece of embroidery, usually worn with church vestments, named for Phrygia in Asia Minor, an ancient kingdom where such embroidery was done in gold thread. Orphreys were often worked on separate bands of material that could be worn with different garments, like jewelry.

## osnaburg or osnabruk

A coarse heavy fabric of linen or cotton, named for the industrial city of Osnabrück, West Germany, where it originated. As a linen, it was used in men's suitings, but in the cotton form woven today it is chiefly an industrial cloth, made into bags and upholstery material.

## paduasoy

A rich, corded silk fabric, used in clothing and upholstery, named for Padua, Italy, since in early days Italy was the only country in Europe where silk was woven. Actually the name is a corruption of the French *pou-de-soie* ("insect of silk").

## pima

A fine strong cotton hybridized from Egyptian and Sea Island plants, named for Pima County, Arizona, where it was developed. Pima is used for balloons, airplane cloths, and tire fabrics.

## poplin

A close-woven, plain-dyed, slightly ribbed cotton, used chiefly in summer raincoats, slacks, and shorts, named *papaline* cloth ("papal") because it originated in Avignon, Vaucluse, France. Avignon was home to the papacy during the so-called Babylonian Captivity (1309–1377).

## Sanforized

An adjective (trademark) meaning preshrunk, applied to linen or cotton, named for Sanford L. Cluett (1874–1968), American clothing manufacturer, who invented this process. Sanforization guarantees that the treated fabric will not shrink more than a quarter inch per yard in either direction.

## satin

Originally, a silk fabric with a shiny front and a dull back, named for Zaytun, the Arabic form of Tsinkiang, where it originated. Today satins are woven of many fibers—cotton, rayon, nylon—and are finished between hot rollers to produce the shiny surface. They are used chiefly in lingerie, formal gowns, and lining materials.

## shalloon

A lightweight woolen twill, used in linings, named for Châlons-sur-Marne, France, where it was woven.

## shantung

A tussah silk (silk woven from the fibers of the wild India tussah moth, a coarser material than that of cultivated silk) with a nubby texture, named for the Chinese province of Shantung, from which it came. Shantung is used in sportswear and summer suits for both men and women.

## stroud

A coarse, heavy woolen material, named for the town of Stroud in Gloucestershire, England, where it was woven. Blanketing made of stroud was once a staple item of trade with the American Indians.

## tabby

A form of taffeta with a moire (wavy-line) finish, named for Attabiya, the district in the city of Baghdad where it was made.

By extension, a cat with a striped or mottled coat is called a tabby cat.

## tattersall

Fancy vesting wool with tartanlike checks and squares, named for Tattersall's horse market in London. Richard Tattersall (1724–1795), who founded the business, sold horse blankets of this material. Hence a tattersall vest has come to symbolize bookmakers, sportsmen, and devotees of racing.

## tulle

Gauze netting material of silk or cotton, named for the town of Tulle, Corrèze, France, where it was supposed to have originated. Actually it was first made in Nottingham, England, on a stocking machine. Tulle was popular in the 1950's for frou-frou evening gowns and is still used in ballet tutus and hat veiling.

## worsted

Smooth, compact yarn made of long fibers—or the fabric woven of it—named for the village of Worthstede (now Worstead) in Norfolkshire, England. Worsted produces such sturdy cloths as serge and gabardine.

# LEATHER . . .

## box calf

Calfskin with square markings, caused by its being rolled both lengthwise and crosswise, named for a London bootmaker, Joseph Box, who developed the technique.

## cordovan

A soft, colored leather, originally made of goatskin but now of split horsehide and pigskin as well, named for Córdoba, Spain, where it was first manufactured. "Cordwain," an English corruption of "cordovan" gives us the word "cordwainer," "shoemaker."

## morocco

A firm pebble-surfaced goatskin, tanned with sumac and usually dyed red, named for the country of its origin. Morocco leather is used in purses, wallets, slippers, and in particularly fine book bindings.

## suede

Leather—originally kidskin but later baby lamb and calfskin as well—buffed with emory cloth to give it a soft velvety nap, named for the French form of "Sweden," where this technique was developed.

# · 8 ·

# Shelter:
# Be It Ever So Humble

Home, today, is often not merely a place to keep warm or out of the rain, but an integral part of one's style of living. Home furnishings and decor vary from country to country, house to house, and are often a reflection of the affluence and culture of the inhabitants.

## CONSTRUCTION STYLES AND TERMS . . .

### attic

A space or area enclosed by the roof framing, usually used as storage space, named for the adjective form of Attica, the province of ancient Greece of which Athens was the capital. In classical architecture, a low wall above the entablature was called an Attic wall and the room behind it, if there was one, an Attic room.

### baroque

A seventeenth-century style (chiefly of architecture but also of other art forms) characterized by elaborate ornamentation, curved lines, and enormous size, named for Federigo Barocci (1528–1612), an Italian painter, whose emotional art was considered to evoke the mood of the reformation.

Perhaps the most grandiose expression of the baroque is St. Peter's Basilica in Rome, an edifice designed on such a vast scale that it covers four acres.

194

## churrigueresque

A Spanish style of baroque architecture, chiefly of churches and cathedrals, named for José Benitode Churriguera (1665–1725), who originated it. Elaborate and artful, characterized by twisted pillars, the style is found in eighteenth-century churches in Spain and many parts of Latin America.

## Gothic

An adjective applied to a medieval style of architecture, characterized by pointed arches, flying buttresses (to support lofty roofs), groined and fan vaulting, and stained glass, named for the Goths, a Teutonic people famed for their wildness. When the Gothic style first appeared (in twelfth-century France), it was regarded as so insane as to be unacceptable to civilized people, hence the name.

## mansard roof

A roof with a double pitch, the lower so steep as to be nearly vertical, the upper with a shallow slope, named for French architect François Mansart (1598–1666), who is credited with having invented it.

The lower slope of the roof, fitted with dormer windows, forms an additional story to the house, and the tale is that in the seventeenth century Parisian householders were taxed according to the number of stories they had "under the roof." Mansard designed his roof so that the owner could have an additional story without paying an increase in taxes.

## Palladian window

A window treatment in which a central window with a round-arch top is flanked by two square-topped windows, named for Italian architect Andrea Palladio (1518–1580). In Europe only very grand buildings, as a rule, display Palladian windows, but many American private homes (of the colonial period or a style imitating it) have them, usually on the second floor above the entrance.

## Romanesque

An adjective applied to a style of architecture characterized by round arches and barrel vaults, named for Rome because it was developed in Italy and is best known for its use in early Christian churches. In England, this style is called Norman because it was brought to the island along with the invasion of William the Conqueror.

## Tudor style

A late-medieval style of architecture characterized by the Tudor arch (a shallow pointed arch) and much interior wood paneling, named for the Tudor family, which ruled England from 1485 to 1603. In America any house with an exterior trim imitating half-timbering (wood framing filled with masonry nogging) is called Tudor.

# SPECIAL STRUCTURES . . .

### coliseum

A large sports amphitheater or exhibition hall, named for the Colosseum of Rome, built by the Emperors Vespasian and Titus and opened in A.D. 79. The Colosseum received its own name from the Colossus, a gigantic statue of Nero which stood in front of it.

### Lady chapel

A small chapel located in or near a cathedral or large church and dedicated to the Virgin Mary, named for her common appellation "Our Lady."

### mausoleum

A tomb with more than one burial site, often belonging to a large family, named for the magnificent white marble tomb of Mausolus, ruler of ancient Caria (now in Turkey), who died in 353 B.C. The original

Mausoleum, 140 feet high and surrounded by thirty-six columns, was one of the seven wonders of the ancient world.

## Nissen hut

A prefabricated hut of corrugated iron, shaped like half a cylinder, named for its designer, Lieutenant Colonel Peter N. Nissen (1871–1930), British mining engineer. Nissen huts, British counterparts to the American Quonset huts, were used chiefly for military shelters during World War II.

## palace

The official residence of a king, president, bishop, or other notable, named for the Palatine Hill in Rome, where the residences of various emperors were built.

## pantechnicon

A British term for a large storage warehouse, named for the nineteenth-century Pantechnicon, a bazaar at which art objects were sold.

## pantheon

A building containing memorials to a nation's famous men and/or war dead, named for the Pantheon in Rome, built by Agrippa in 25 B.C. The Greek word means something like "building dedicated to all gods" and originally denoted a temple, but it has come to mean a national shrine.

The Roman Pantheon, though looted and neglected during the Middle Ages, has survived, and since the Renaissance several noted Italians have been buried there, including the artist Raphael.

## Quonset hut

Trademark name for a prefabricated hut of corrugated metal, named for Quonset Point, Rhode Island, where it was manufactured.

Quonset huts, easily erected, sturdy, and reasonably well insulated against weather extremes, saw service in all theaters of World War II, but perhaps their most memorable use was as temporary postwar housing. On university campuses, swamped with GI Bill students, Quonsets sprang up like mushrooms—and vanished just as quickly when the need for them was past.

# SPECIAL PLACES . . .

## Hooverville

A shantytown, composed of makeshift shelters and located usually on wasteland or some other undesirable location, named for Herbert Clark Hoover (1874–1964), thirty-first American President.

Hoover did not bring on the Great Depression, but he did little to relieve the misery it caused, and his name has become a pejorative term for hard times. Hoover blankets were newspapers wrapped around the body to keep warm. Hoover carts were old ramshackle automobiles pulled by mules. Hoover flags were pockets turned inside out to show that they were empty. And "to Hooverize" meant to economize by saving on food.

## mall

A public area, either an outdoor, tree-lined promenade for strolling or an indoor shopping street, named for The Mall in St. James Park, London, a famous walk in the seventeenth century. The Mall itself derives its name from the game pall-mall, played with a wooden ball and mallets, for which it was originally laid out as an alley.

## podunk

A jerkwater town, small and usually rural, named for the village of Podunk, near Worcester, Massachusetts. Nobody knows why people began to settle on this inoffensive community as the symbol of isolation and small-town narrow-mindedness, but the name has persisted.

## ritzy

Flamboyantly fashionable and ostentatiously expensive, named for the Ritz hotels, founded in many cities by Swiss-born Cesar Ritz (1850–1918). The elegant Ritz hotels soon became a byword for luxurious living, and "to put on the Ritz" meant to attempt to outshine others with a dazzling display of wealth or social position.

## spa

A resort community containing a mineral spring, named for the town of Spa in Belgium, known since the time of the Romans. Two of Spa's many famous visitors were Czar Peter the Great and Kaiser Wilhelm II.

# IDEAL COMMUNITIES . . .

## arcadia

A place of rural peace and tranquillity, named for the ancient province of Arkadia in central Peloponnesus, Greece, an isolated pastoral region.

## Camelot

A time or place of ideal happiness, usually seen in retrospect, named for the city of King Arthur and his Round Table in the Arthurian legend. The term has been given new life in recent decades by the Lerner and Loewe musical *Camelot*, based on T.H. White's novel *The Once and Future King*.

For a few years in the late 1960's, young followers of the Kennedy family liked to refer to President John F. Kennedy's years in office (1960–1963) as Camelot, because on looking back, it seemed to be a period of hope and promise.

## cloud-cuckoo-land

A realm of fantasy, usually eccentrically conceived, named for the fictional country in Aristophanes' *The Birds*. To be away off in cloud-cuckoo-land is to be out of touch with reality.

## Elysium

A state of idyllic happiness (not usually thought of as an actual place but as a condition of mind), named for the mythological afterworld of ancient Greece and Rome, where happy souls dwelled. It is sometimes also called the Elysian Fields, and this form of the name has been applied by the French to the graceful Parisian avenue that leads up to the Arc de Triomphe, *les Champs Elysées*.

## Garden of Eden

Any place of beauty and happiness, specifically one surrounded by the bounties of nature and removed from worldly cares, named for the biblical paradise in which Adam and Eve were originally placed:

> And the Lord God planted a garden eastward in Eden . . .
> And out of the ground made the Lord God to grow every
> tree that is pleasant to the sight, and good for food . . .
> (Genesis 2:8–9)

The name "Eden" came from the Hebrew word for "delight."

## Shangri-La

A distant, perhaps unattainable land of perpetual youth toward which one is drawn even though it means a long struggle, named for the remote Himalayan paradise in James Hilton's novel *Lost Horizon*. *La* is actually the Tibetan word for "mountain pass."

## Utopia

A place of ideal government and social conditions, named for the island community in Sir Thomas More's political romance *Utopia*. The name is a transliteration of the Greek word for "no place." On Utopia, there was equal education for both men and women, religious freedom, a six-hour workday, and the right to change jobs freely if boredom set in—all considered wild-eyed fantasies in Sir Thomas' day.

# RELIGIOUS CENTERS . . .

### bethel

Any house of worship, specifically a chapel or meetinghouse for a nonconformist sect, named for the biblical town where Jacob set up an altar. Jacob, son of Isaac, saw in a dream a vision of angels going up and down a ladder that led to heaven. At the top was the Lord, who said:

> I am the Lord God of Abraham, thy father, and the God of Isaac: the land whereon thou liest, to thee will I give it, and to thy seed. (Genesis 28:13)

When Jacob arose in the morning, he set up an altar and called the place *beth-El*, "House of God."

### mecca

The goal, the symbol of highest achievement in some field, named for the holiest city of Islam, the birthplace of the prophet Muhammad.

Millions of Muslims bow their heads in the direction of Mecca in Saudi Arabia when they pray, as they are required to do five times a day. And at least once in a lifetime, if possible, they make a pilgrimage to this "Mother of Cities."

# FURNISHINGS . . .

### amboyna

A reddish-brown wood, one of the many tropical furniture materials labeled "rosewood," named for the island of Amboina in the Moluccas, Indonesia, from which it comes.

## calamander

A hard furniture wood whose grain gives a striped effect, named for the Coromandel Coast of India, where it is found.

The Coromandel is the lower eastern coast of the subcontinent, centered on Madras; the lower western coast is called the Malabar.

## chesterfield

An overstuffed sofa with upright arm rests, named for a nineteenth-century earl of Chesterfield, perhaps to give it an air of elegance.

## davenport

Originally a small writing table with drawers, later a sofa (often one that can be converted into a bed), named for a nineteenth-century English manufacturer, a Mr. Davenport.

## Hitchcock chair

A rush-seated, slat-backed chair, painted (usually black) and decorated with stenciled designs, named for its manufacturer, Lambert H. Hitchcock (1795–1852). The Hitchcock is probably the first mass-produced American chair.

## Jenny Lind bed

A wooden spool bed, named for the Swedish Nightingale, Jenny Lind-Goldschmidt (1820–1887), a magnificent coloratura soprano. Lind toured America in the 1850's under the auspices of P.T. Barnum, and was so popular that her name alone was probably enough to make furniture sell.

## Morris chair

A chair designed specifically for comfort, usually one with an adjustable back, removable cushions, and straight wooden arms, named for English poet-artist William Morris (1834–1896), who designed it.

Morris, although primarily a writer and illustrator, had many diverse interests, including typography, dyeing and carpet weaving, medieval buildings, and interior decoration. He was the virtual founder of the handicrafts movement. He began to design furniture after he moved into a London flat and found difficulty in getting the right furnishings to suit his tastes. Later he designed and built his own house.

Despite his many talents, however, his name is most undetachably linked with this chair. It is often considered the first chair built wholly for comfort.

## Murphy bed

A bed that folds up into a closet against the wall, named for its inventor William L. Murphy (1876–1950). In the early days of small (especially one-room) apartments, the Murphy bed was a godsend, and it provided silent movies with endless comic material by its flair for folding up with the occupant still inside.

## ottoman

A large footstool or backless seat, well stuffed, named for the Ottoman Empire (now Turkey) because it was thought to resemble Near Eastern divans.

## Windsor chair

An all-wooden chair with a concave seat, spindle back, and outward slanting legs, named for Windsor Castle, residence of British monarchs for many centuries, near which it was first made in the eighteenth century.

The back on a Windsor chair may have any of several different forms—an arch shape, a straight top, a double-level comb back, etc.

# WALL AND WINDOW TREATMENTS . . .

## arras

Wall hanging with a pictorial design, of Flemish origin but named for the town of Arras, Pas de Calais, France.

If Shakespeare is to be believed, arrases were favorite places of concealment, from behind which one could overhear plotting. They are employed thus in *The Merry Wives of Windsor, Much Ado About Nothing, King John, Henry IV* Part I, and *Hamlet.*

## cremone lock

A lock for use on double doors or casement windows, consisting of rods that move up and down to engage matching holes in the frame, top and bottom, named for Cremona, Lombardy, Italy, where it originated.

## Gobelin

A variety of hand-woven tapestry, named for Gilles and Jehan Gobelin, a family of French dyers, who established the business in the fifteenth century. The Gobelin factory was made a royal establishment by Louis XIV and is now nationalized.

Gobelins have given their name to several shades of color and to the Gobelin stitch, a background stitch worked slantwise.

## valance

A short drapery, sometimes elaborately flounced or festooned, often of wood or padded with upholstery, used to conceal the tops of draperies or the underpinnings of a couch, named for the town of Valence, Tarn-et-Garonne, France, a textile manufacturing center.

## venetian blinds

A window made up of horizontal slats connected by twill straps and so arranged that they can be opened or closed by pulling a cord, named for the city of Venice, Italy.

# RUGS AND CARPETS . . .

## Aubusson

A wool or silk rug without pile, woven with floral or scroll designs in imitation of Aubusson tapestries, named for Aubusson, Creuse, France, where the tapestry originated.

During the Middle Ages weavers were brought to this region from Flanders to produce tapestries for the local nobility, and the craft was soon established in the area.

## Kidderminster

A variety of ingrain carpet (carpet woven of predyed wool so that the same design appears on both sides, only with colors reversed), named for the town of Kidderminster in Worcestershire, England, where the original is manufactured.

## Konia

A Turkish rug woven in soft shades of the primary colors, named for the town of Konia, Turkey.

## Oriental rug

A woolen carpet of great beauty and durability and intricate design (said to have been an attempt originally to bring the garden indoors), woven and knotted by hand. It is named Oriental because it is made in the Near East.

Oriental rugs come in many different types and styles and are variously labeled "Persian rug" or "Turkey carpet" depending on the land in which they were made. The art form is an exacting one, employing many women and children because their small hands make them defter than men at tying the special knots, but it may be dying out. As oil money flows into Asia Minor, creating industry, would-be carpet weavers are attracted into easier, better-paying factory jobs.

# Part 4

---

# INTELLECT AND ENTERTAINMENT

# · 9 ·

# Literature:
# The World of Words

Our progress is dependent upon our ability to exchange information and pass knowledge from generation to generation. Historically, this has been done by word of mouth, through cave drawings, on Mesopotamian clay tablets, on Egyptian tomb walls, in Greek and Roman scrolls, through Gutenberg's movable type, and with IBM's computers.

Literature, whether for technical or amusement purposes, is an important means of communication that can satisfy a variety of human needs.

## BOOKS AND VERSE . . .

### Bible

A definitive and authoritative reference work, whose word is more or less law within its field, named for Holy Scriptures.

The Bible itself derives its name from the Greek word for "book," but that in turn probably came from the Phoenician port of Byblos (now Jubayl, Lebanon), whence papyrus, the earliest paper, was exported to the rest of the Mediterranean world.

The Old Testament of the Bible is much larger than the New, containing thirty-nine books to twenty-seven for the New Testament, 929 chapters to 260, and 592,439 words to 181,253.

### English sonnet

An Italian sonnet with slightly changed rhyme scheme, which sums up its point with a strong rhyming couplet at the end, named English because it was developed by a number of different sixteenth-century English poets, including Shakespeare.

## euphuism

An affected style of writing or speaking, employing elaborate and contrived literary forms, named for the fictional Euphues, the hero of two romances by John Lyly (1554–1606): *Euphues, the Anatomy of Wit* and *Euphues and His England.* Euphuism was a popular rage in England throughout the 1580's, but it was so easily parodied that it soon fell out of favor.

Today the term is applied chiefly to work that attempts, but does not achieve, elegance.

## glyconic

A rhythmic pattern or verse form, named for its purported inventor, Glycon, a Greek poet of unknown date. Horace and Catullus, lyric poets of the first century B.C., sometimes employed the glyconic form.

## Gongorism

A convoluted and artificial style of writing, named for the Spanish poet Luis de Góngora by Argote (1561–1627). Góngora specialized in studied obscurity and complicated literary devices.

## Horatian ode

An ode (a lyric poem devoted to praise of someone or something) in stanza form, each stanza following the pattern of the first, which may take any form the author chooses, named for the Roman poet Quintus Horatius Flaccus (65–8 B.C.), who developed it.

English poets of the Romantic Period often wrote lyrics in the form of the Horatian ode.

## Italian sonnet

A fourteen-line poem written according to strict rhyme-scheme rules, named Italian because it was invented by Guittone of Arezzo in the thirteenth century. It is divided into octave (first eight lines) and sestet (last six lines), and the break between the two marks a break in the author's thought pattern.

The Italian sonnet is sometimes called the Petrarchan sonnet because it was favored by the Arezzan poet Francesco Petrarca (1304–1374).

## Pindaric ode

An ode in units of three stanzas each (strophe, antistrophe, and epode), named for the Greek poet Pindar (522–443 B.C.), who composed such odes in celebration of the victors in the Isthmian and Olympic Games.

# LITERARY TERMS . . .

## bowdlerize

A verb meaning "to subject a literary work to ruthless expurgation"—originally of prurient material but later of passages considered too strongly stated—named for Thomas Bowdler (1754–1825), an English editor.

Bowdler believed that material should not be put into books "which cannot with propriety be read in a family," and he followed this line when he "cleansed" such works as the Old Testament, Gibbon's *Decline and Fall,* and Shakespeare's plays.

## Canterbury tale

A long, rambling, and tedious story, named for the tales told by Geoffrey Chaucer's fictional pilgrims in *The Canterbury Tales.*

## clerihew

A quatrain of light verse consisting of two rhyming couplets, in which some well-known person is mentioned and then humorously discussed, named for Edmund Clerihew Bentley (1875–1956), who invented the form:

> Sir Christopher Wren
> Said, "I am going to dine with some men.
> If anyone calls
> Say I am designing St. Paul's."

Bentley's principal occupation was writing detective stories, his best-known novel being *Trent's Last Case.*

## comstockery

Prudish hunting out of immorality (alleged or actual) in literary works, named for Anthony Comstock (1844–1915), self-appointed censor of books and pictures. The term was invented by George Bernard Shaw.

Comstock, as founder and secretary of the New York Society for the Suppression of Vice, led many campaigns against abortion, birth control, and pornography. He was instrumental in preventing certain types of literature from being sent through the mails, and it is estimated that he was responsible for the arrest of more than three thousand persons—not to mention the destruction of tons of books and millions of pictures.

## grangerize

A verb meaning "to add illustrations to a book," usually by mutilating other books, named for the English writer and print collector James Granger (1723–1776).

Granger wrote *The Biographical History of England* and left blank pages for readers to add illustrations of the various subjects as they found them. Presumably he intended this as an encouragement to making collections of portrait prints, but it resulted in readers' cutting illustrations out of other books in order to complete Granger's.

## Grub Street

The career of literary hack, named for Grub (now Milton) Street in London, where writers of dictionaries, poems, and small histories lived in the eighteenth century. "To live on Grub Street" means to support oneself by literary odd jobs.

## hack

A writer who writes what publishers want written rather than material of his own devising, named in roundabout fashion for the village of Hackney near London.

The original hacks were driving horses (raised in pastures near Hackney), hired out to the public, and from there the term came to be applied to anyone (political hacks, for example) who did unimaginative work at someone else's behest.

## malapropism

Humorous substitution of one word for another, similar in sound but quite different in meaning, named for the fictional Mrs. Malaprop in Richard Brinsley Sheridan's play *The Rivals*. "Are you casting asparagus on my character?" is a malapropism, as is "Achilles' mother dipped him in the River Stinx until he was intolerable."

## spoonerism

An accidental slip of the tongue that transposes the sounds (usually consonants) of two words to produce a ludicrous distortion of what the speaker intended to say, named for William Archibald Spooner (1844–1930), who was prone to this kind of lapse.

As dean of New College, Oxford, Spooner and his slips became famous among students, who soon spread the word far and wide. Many of those now attributed to him were invented by others, and the form is popular enough that entire books of humor have been written in spoonerisms.

"Let me sew you to your sheet" is a spoonerism, as is "Deal him a blushing crow." Dr. Spooner's own best-known lapse was made on the occasion of his announcing the hymn to be sung at church services: "Kinquering Congs Their Titles Take."

The history of radio and television is full of memorable spoonerisms: "We are the world's largest manufacturers of magnoosium, aleeminum, and stool." "Cast your broad upon the waters. This is the National Breadcasting Company." And the one that immortalized the hapless Harry Von Zell: "Ladies and gentlemen, the President of the United States, Hoobert Heever."

# BOOKMAKING . . .

## braille

A system of writing for the blind, consisting of patterns of raised dots, named for its inventor, Louis Braille (1809–1852).

Many techniques had been tried for teaching the blind to read before Braille's day, but most (see *Moon type*) were based on the visual alphabet, not quickly identifiable by touch. But Louis Braille, blind himself, devised a system specifically geared to touch—dots arranged in variations of six positions—and it has been so successful that it has come into use for the blind around the world.

Today, special devices enable the blind to take notes and typewrite in braille, to play games with braille cards, and to read braille menus.

## Gothic

A term used for two different kinds of typeface, either black letter ("Olde Englishe") or sans serif, named after the Gothic style of architecture and art (see Chapter 8, Construction Styles and Terms). Both forms of Gothic are hard to read and hence are rarely used for text type. But on title pages and in headlines, they are useful for achieving special typographical effects.

## India ink

A black permanent ink used with a very fine pen in drawing and lettering, named India because it was thought to come from there:

Actually India ink originated in China, where calligraphy has been developed into a true art form.


## Italian hand

A round, clear, slightly slanting handwriting, named Italian because it was developed in Italy during the twelfth century. The kind of typeface called italics is an attempt to reproduce Italian hand in printing.

The phrase "fine Italian hand" has become synonymous with devious underhandedness, probably from the bad reputation of Renaissance politics in Italy.


## italics

A light, sloping form of a typeface, named for the Italian handwriting it originally attempted to imitate.

In the early days of printing, whole books were reproduced in italics—the first being a book published in Venice in 1501—and as late as the early nineteenth century, prefaces and other front matter still frequently appeared entirely in this form.

Today the uses of italics, though narrower, are essential in typesetting. Most standard roman typefaces have italic forms in matching fonts, so that italics can be used to indicate emphasis, specify book titles and foreign words, and serve other such special purposes. In typesetting a manuscript, all underlined words are set in italic type, the balance in roman.


## Kufic

An angular decorative form of Arabic writing, used only for making copies of the Koran and for coins and monuments, named for Kufa on the Euphrates River in Iraq, where it was developed by Arabian calligraphers in the seventh century.


## levant

A leather of the Morocco type of sheep-, goat-, or sealskin with a drawn-grain pattern, named for the Levant nations (those at the eastern end of the Mediterranean), where it originated. It is used in bookbinding.

## Moon type

An alphabet of raised letters, used by blind people unable to master braille, named for William Moon (1818–1894), the Englishman who invented it.

Moon type is based on the visual alphabet, much simplified (since touch is too crude to distinguish differences plainly visible to the eye), and is thus of great help to persons blinded late in life, whose fingers may be too stiff or insensitive to learn braille. But Moon has many drawbacks. It takes up much more space than braille, it is far slower to read, and it cannot be used by the blind for writing.

## Palmer method

A large and flowing style of handwriting, widely taught in American schools, named for Austin Norman Palmer (1859–1927), who developed it.

## parchment

The inner hide of a sheep or goat, dried and scraped and smoothed, used as a substitute for paper, named for the medieval English word for "pergamum." This ancient kingdom (now western Turkey) is supposedly the place where the use of animal skin as a substitute for papyrus was invented.

Throughout the Middle Ages, until the spread of papermaking (which did not reach Europe until the twelfth century), parchment was the primary material for the making of books and documents. Even today it is sometimes employed for charters, treaties, or other important papers. A specially fine variety of parchment, made from calfskin, is called vellum.

## roman

Standard form of typeface with serifs (short appendage lines stemming from the main part of a typeface), named Roman because ancient

Roman monuments and manuscripts were inscribed in similarly shaped letters. This book is set in Times Roman, a roman face.

## solander

A protective box for books or documents, sometimes made in the shape of a book itself, named for Daniel C. Solander (1736–1782), a Swedish botanist. Solander, who traveled to England to instruct naturalists in Linnaeus' system of botanical classification, was hired to catalog the natural-history collection of the British Museum and invented the solander as an aid to storing fragile or miscellaneous material.

## Spencerian

A delicate, slanted form of American handwriting, popular in the nineteenth century, named for Platt Rogers Spencer (1800–1864), who developed the original form and introduced it to schools and business colleges. Spencerian was generally superseded by the graceful and more legible Palmer method.

# · 10 ·

# Entertainment: Music, Art, Sports, and Other Diversions

In our hectic world, a great deal of time is taken up providing for our basic needs. But we must have our moments of relaxation as well, and for them the concert hall and the art gallery, the sports arena and the amusement park provide pleasure and support for the human spirit.

## MUSIC IN ALL ITS FORMS . . .

### music

The art of producing pleasing sounds, named for the Muses of classical Greek mythology. In its original sense the term "musical" was applied to any art presided over by one of the nine Muses. In time it came to refer only to an aural art form.

The Muses were the daughters of Zeus and Mnemosyne (Memory), thought to live in the neighborhood of springs, particularly those at the feet of Mount Helicon, Olympus, and Parnassus, from which artists and poets could derive inspiration by drinking. These are the nine: Calliope ("beautiful voice"), muse of epic poetry; Clio ("the extoller"), muse of history; Euterpe ("the one who gladdens"), muse of lyric song; Thalia ("the one who flourishes"), muse of comedy; Melpomene ("the singer"), muse of tragedy; Terpsichore ("she who rejoices in the dance"), the muse of dancing; Erato ("the lovely"), the muse of love poetry; Polymnia ("she who is rich in hymns"), the muse of sacred songs; and Urania ("the heavenly"), the muse of astronomy.

# MUSICAL INSTRUMENTS . . .

## calliope

A musical instrument consisting of a series of steam whistles tuned to the notes of the scale and played by means of a keyboard, named for the muse of epic poetry (see *music*).

The calliope is extremely loud—it can sometimes be heard ten miles away—which made it an ideal instrument for circuses and showboats to announce their arrivals. It was invented in 1855 by Joshua C. Stoddard of Worcester, Massachusetts.

## jew's harp

A small cheap, metallic instrument, played by holding the metal rim between the teeth and twanging the flexible metal tongue, named perhaps because it was sold by Jewish peddlers. Other explanations for the name are that it was a corruption of "jaw's harp" or of the Dutch *jeugdharp*, "boy's harp."

The jew's harp is a very old instrument, played in Scotland before the bagpipe. It was also popular among American Indians and became an important item in the early fur trade. It was not unusual to encounter a hunter returning from the trading post, magnificent in feathers and paint, solemnly twanging on his newly acquired jew's harp.

## panpipes

A primitive instrument consisting of a graduated series of flageolets, each representing a note of the scale, bound together and played by moving the mouth from hole to hole, named for the Greek god of woods and shepherds, who was supposed to have invented it.

According to the myth, Pan fell in love with nymph Syrinx and pursued her. When she reached the bank of the River Ladon (now the Ladhon) in the Peloponnesus, she prayed for help and was changed into marsh reeds. Pan heard the wind blowing through them and, charmed with the sound, cut a bundle of them and fashioned the panpipes.

## pantaleon

A huge dulcimer, eleven feet long with 250 strings of gut and metal, named for its inventor Pantaleon Hebenstreit (1669–1750), a German musician.

Hebenstreit composed a number of overtures and concertos for the pantaleon, but it was too unwieldly to become popular.

## sarrusophone

A double-reed metal wind instrument with a wide bore and a narrow mouthpiece, played somewhat like a bassoon and sometimes substituted for it, named for a nineteenth-century French bandmaster named Sarrus. Like the sousaphone, it is more often found in military bands than in concert orchestras.

## saxophone

A family of metal reed instruments with a tube that curves up and out, named for their inventor Adolphe Sax (1814–1894), a Belgian instrument maker. Sax also invented the saxhorn and the saxotrumba.

The saxophone is primarily an instrument for pop music of various sorts. The alto and tenor saxophone are occasionally used in symphonic music and often in military bands, but the baritone, bass, and soprano saxes are rarely heard except in pop music groups. The saxophone is not played in true primitive jazz but is a sophisticated addition.

## sousaphone

A bass tuba with a very large bell, made in circular form to be worn over the player's shoulders, named for the American bandmaster and composer John Philip Sousa (1854–1932). The sousaphone is particularly well adapted to the needs of a marching band, and in the United States has virtually ousted the normal tuba from military and school bands.

Sousa, the March King, who began his musical career at the age of thirteen when he joined the U.S. Marine Band as a trombonist, composed some 140 military marches—including such classics as "The

Stars and Stripes Forever," "Semper Fidelis," and "The Washington Post"—plus eleven operettas. He also wrote three novels and an autobiography.

## spinet

Originally a small harpsichord, now a small upright piano, named for the fifteenth-century Italian instrument maker Giovanni Spinetti.

## theremin

A melodic electronic instrument named for its inventor, Russian engineer Leon Theremin (b. 1896).

## ukulele

Four-stringed guitarlike plucking/strumming instrument, named for the Hawaiian nickname of Edward Purvis, British army officer stationed in the Hawaiian Islands in the 1880s. *Ukulele* means "small jumping person," and the name was bestowed on Purvis for his liveliness. He discovered the instrument there—probably the descendant of a guitar left behind by some early Portuguese seaman—and popularized its use. The name was patented by the Honolulu Ad Club in 1917.

# DANCES . . .

## apache dance

A violent, somewhat acrobatic dance favored by members of the nineteenth-century French underworld, named apaches by French journalist Émile Darsy.

## Charleston

A kind of two-step in which the heels are swung out to the side, named for the city of Charleston, South Carolina, where the dance originated. So popular did the Charleston become in the 1920's that it is regarded as the dance symbol of that decade.


## conga

A humorous dance in which the dancers line up one behind the other and then one-two-three-kick in unison, named for the Afro-Cuban conga drum. The dance, though African in name, was invented in Cuba in the 1930's.


## flamenco

A flamboyant dance of Andalusian gypsy origin, characterized by colorful costumes, hand clapping, foot stamping, and sensuous postures, named for the Spanish form of "Flemish." The Spaniards apply this term to the gypsy people of this region.


## lindy

A basic jitterbug step, originating in Harlem in the late 1920's and named for the current popular hero, Charles Augustus Lindbergh (1902–1974). Lindbergh made the first nonstop solo transatlantic flight on May 20–21, 1927.


## malagueña

A paired dance, usually to the accompaniment of a folk tune and castanets, named for the city of Málaga in southern Spain, near which it originated.


## mazurka

A folk dance characterized by a slide and a hop to one side, named for the Mazurs, a Protestant sect of southeastern Prussia (now part of Poland). Frédéric Chopin, the great Polish-born composer, wrote more than fifty mazurkas for the piano.

## morris

A vigorous kind of traditional story dance, which is performed by costumed dancers with blackened faces and bells, usually at established pageants and celebrations, named for the Moors of Spain. Morris dancing was introduced into England from Spain in the fourteenth century, and the blackened faces represent the dark complexions of the original performers.

A famous solo performance of the morris was carried out by one William Kemp, a contemporary of Shakespeare. He danced the morris from London to Norwich, and for his marathon effort he was awarded a pension of forty shillings a year.

## polka

A folk-dance step consisting of three steps and a hop, introduced and popularized in the 1840's, and named for the Czechoslovakian word for "Pole."

This lively dance is actually native to Bohemia (now Czechoslovakia), but it is regarded by Poles as their native dance. Many famous composers of the nineteenth century have composed music in a polka beat, and it is second only to the waltz in its lasting popularity.

## polonaise

A stately dance in three-quarter time, dating back at least to the sixteenth century, named for the French form of "Polish." In the nineteenth century, it was used as a processional dance, in which couples marched around the ball room in promenade. It is rarely performed today as a dance, but music for it—by such masters as Bach, Beethoven, Handel, and Mussorgsky—is still popular. Chopin's thirteen polonaises constitute a stirring repertoire for the piano.

## rigadoon

A lively dance performed with a jumping step in two-quarter or four-quarter time, named for a dancing master in Marseille, a Monsieur Rigaud, who invented it.

## tarantella

A lively Italian dance in six-eighth time, named for Taranto in southern Italy. (See *tarantula*.)

## Virginia reel

The American form of the English country dance called the Roger de Coverly, named for the Commonwealth of Virginia. Four couples pair off in two lines facing one another, meet to perform certain country-dance steps, and move up gradually to the head of the line.

# OTHER FORMS OF MUSIC . . .

## calypso

An improvisational form of ballad, developed and perfected by West Indian blacks, named for the mythological nymph Calypso, who retained Odysseus on her island for seven years.

Calypso music satirizes current events or popular tales and is one of the Caribbean's principal contributions to world culture.

## Gregorian chant

Plainsong, church music consisting of a single line of vocal melody without accompaniment and without formal rhythm (not set in bars or time), named for Saint Gregory the Great (Pope Gregory I) (540–604), under whose auspices it was introduced.

# ART . . .

## Maecenas

A patron of art and/or artists, usually on a munificent scale, named for Gaius Cilnius Maecenas (70–8 B.C.), Roman statesman and counsel-

or to the Emperor Augustus. Maecenas profoundly influenced the two greatest poets of Latin literature, Virgil and Horace.

## silhouette

A kind of picture in which the subject is seen only in outline, the body of the image being filled in with a solid color, usually black, named for Étienne de Silhouette (1709–1767), controller general of finances under Louis XV.

Silhouette attempted to introduce economies into the French government, principally by doing away with the pensions and privileges of the nobility. His hobby was cutting portraits of people out of paper, and when the fashion for silhouette art came in, the French nobles jeeringly called it *art à la Silhouette*—or art "on the cheap."

# COLORS . . .

## alice blue

A light, slightly grayish blue, stronger than forget-me-not blue, named for Alice Roosevelt Longworth, daughter of President Theodore Roosevelt (b. 1884).

## celadon

A grayish yellow-green, named for the mooning lover Celadon in Honore d'Urfe's pastoral romance *L'Astree*.

## chartreuse

A brilliant yellow green, named for the Carthusian monastery of Grand Chartreuse, near Grenoble, Isère, France, which developed the famous liqueur of that color still called chartreuse.

## cudbear

A red or purplish coloring matter obtained from lichens, named for Cuthbert Gordon, a Scottish chemist who patented it in the eighteenth century.

## davy's gray

Steel gray, named for the English chemist Sir Humphrey Davy (1778–1829), who is chiefly remembered for the miners' safety lamp he invented.

## iridescent

An adjective applied to anything which shows changing color effects with different plays of light, named for the mythological Iris, Greek goddess of the rainbow.

## Lincoln green

A moderate olive green, named for the city of Lincoln, England, where it originated. Lincoln green was favored by foresters, perhaps because it enabled them to blend more readily with the greenery around them, but it is best known for its association with Robin Hood.

## maclura

The bright-orange color of the wood of the osage orange tree, named for William Maclure (1763–1840), Scottish-American geologist.

## magenta

A dark purplish red, made from a coal-tar dye called fuchsine, named for the Battle of Magenta, fought near the town in Lombardy of the same name on June 4, 1859. Seven thousand French and Austrian troops were killed and their bodies buried in a common vault. When, shortly after this clash, the dye was discovered, its inventor named it magenta for the great quantities of blood spilled there.

## Prussian blue

A strong, medium-dark blue, named Prussian because the well-disciplined armies of Prussia wore uniforms of this shade.

## sienna

A reddish-brown color, named for the city of Siena, Tuscany, Italy, near which the clay that yielded it was originally found. When calcined, sienna becomes more reddish in color and is then called burnt sienna.

## titian

A brownish red, nearly always applied to hair color, named for the painter Titian (Tiziano Vecellio) (1477–1576), who often used this shade for hair color in his paintings.

## turquoise

A bluish green, named for the French form of "Turkish," since the mineral turquoise was first discovered in Turkestan, a region in Central Asia that is now part of the Soviet Union.

## Tyrian purple

A purplish-red dye obtained from a marine snail of the genus Thais, named for the city of Tyre in ancient Phoenicia (now Lebanon), from which it was shipped all over the Mediterranean and beyond.

So rare and valuable was this rich dye that wearing it was the prerogative of kings, nobles, and aristocrats.

## Vandyke red

A grayish red, named for Sir Anthony Van Dyke, the Flemish portraitist who favored it in his paintings. A shade of deep brown is also named for Vandyke.

# SPORTS . . .

## Australian crawl

An overarm swimming stroke accompanied by foot kicking, named "Australian" because it was introduced into England in 1902 from Australia. Actually it had long been used by Pacific Islanders. Accompanied by the flutter kick, introduced by Duke Kahanamoku in the 1912 Olympics, it is far and away the fastest of all swimming strokes.

## axel

A skating term named for Axel Paulsen, a Norwegian figure skater who invented it in the 1890's.

An axel is a graceful jump from the outer forward edge of one skate with 1½ turns in the air followed by return to the outer back edge of the other skate. Accomplished figure skaters often perform double or triple axels.

## badminton

A court game played with long-handled rackets and a shuttlecock, named for the estate of the eighth duke of Beaufort, where it was first played in England. The game originated in India and from there was carried by British officers to their homeland.

## Baltimore chop

In baseball, a hard-hit ball that bounces over the head of an infielder, named for the city of Baltimore.

## canter

A brisk three-beat gait of a horse, faster than a trot but slower than a gallop, named canterbury gallop—canter for short—because it was a favorite pace for pilgrims riding to Canterbury and other shrines.

## Chicago

A variety of rotation pool (that is, where the balls are played in their numerical order) in which at the start of the game the balls are placed around the edge of the table, named for the city of Chicago.

## christiania (or christy)

In skiing a high-speed turn, executed by parallel skis, named for the former name of Oslo, the Norwegian capital.

## derby

Any important race held annually and restricted (usually) to three-year-old horses, named for the Derby Stakes, established at Epsom Downs in Surrey, England, in 1780. The Derby Stakes themselves were named for their founder, Edward Stanley, twelfth earl of Derby.

## English billiards

A game played on a table with six pockets, in which scores are made by cannons and pocketed balls, named "English" for its popularity in England.

## Garrison finish

A last-minute victory in a horse race by an animal who comes up from behind, named for Edward H. ("Snapper") Garrison (1868–1930), an American jockey, who used this technique for winning the Suburban Handicap in 1892.

## Jackson Haines

In figure skating a sit-spin, in which the performer, while spinning, gradually lowers his body to a sitting posture, with one leg extended, then slowly rises, named for the American figure-skating artist of the same name (1840–1879). Haines, a Canadian-born American dancer who studied figure skating in Vienna, applied dancing techniques to what had been an idle pastime and virtually created the modern sport.

## jinete

Someone who trains raw colts to the saddle, named for the Zenetes, a Berber tribe of North Africa, who were skilled horsemen. (See *jennet.*)

## Maggie's drawers

In target shooting, a red flag waved to indicate that a shot has entirely missed the target, named for some unknown Maggie.

## marathon

A footrace of 26 miles 385 yards, named for the ancient battle of Marathon (490 B.C.) at which the Athenians defeated an invading army of Persians. The runner who carried the good news to Athens had just enough time to gasp out, *"Chairete, nikomen!"* ("Rejoice, we are victorious!") and then dropped dead.

Emulation of this famous run was introduced into the revived Olympic Games in 1896 and won by a Greek, and it has figured in every holding of the Games since then. The actual distance, however, is not that of Marathon to Athens, as one might expect, but that of Windsor Castle to White City Stadium, where the 1908 Games were held. It was arranged that way to enable a royal personage to open the race and was officially standardized at that distance in 1924.

## martingale

A strap to prevent a horse from tossing his head and getting the bit in his teeth, named for the village of Martigues, Bouches-du-Rhone,

France, where local men had a particular way of tying up their pants. The martingale runs from the girth, between the animal's front legs, to the bridle or (a running martingale) to the reins.

## rugby

An offshoot of soccer played with fifteen players and an oval ball, in which the ball may be thrown and caught with the hands, named for Rugby School, Rugby in Warwickshire, England, where the game originated. It is said to have had its start in 1823 during a game of soccer when a student player, William Webb Ellis, held the ball (against the rules) and then ran with it.

Rugby is the parent of American football, although the latter has deviated considerably from the relatively gentle rugby.

## Russian roulette

Not a sport at all but a dangerous juvenile game in which a revolver with one bullet is held to the head, the barrel spun, and the trigger pulled, named "Russian" because Czarist officers, when drunk, were sometimes led to challenge one another to take such a foolish risk.

## telemark

In skiing a curving turn made with one ski ahead of the other, named for Telemark, a region in southern Norway, where it was developed in the nineteenth century. Søndre Nordheim (1825–1897), a resident of this area, earned the title "Father of Ski Jumping and Slalom" for his innovative techniques in skiing.

## Texas leaguer

In baseball, a flyball that lands between infield and outfield, usually for a single, named for the minor league of the American Southwest.

## trudgen

In swimming an overarm crawl stroke accompanied by a scissors kick, named for John Trudgen, champion swimmer, who introduced it into England in the 1780's. The trudgen, although not as fast as the later crawl stroke, was considerably speedier than the breast stroke and side stroke, which athletes had been using up until then, and is credited with helping to popularize swimming as a sport.

# CARD GAMES . . .

## faro

A betting game in which players wager which cards they think will be winners, named for the Pharoahs of ancient Egypt, whose picture appeared on early playing cards.

## hoyle

Any authoritative source on the rules for a particular game, named for Edmond Hoyle (1672–1769), whose *A Short Treatise on the Game of Whist* (1742) was the first accepted standard for card and other indoor games.

## Michigan

A complicated betting game in which players wager on a layout of face cards taken from a separate pack, named for the state of Michigan.

## napoleon

A game played with five-card hands in which bids are made on the number of tricks each player expects to make and a chip collected from each of the other players by the winner, named for the Emperor Napoleon, who was prone to collect heavily from those who lost to him, too.

## Newmarket

An English version of Michigan, named for the racing center of Newmarket in Suffolkshire, England.

## Pelmanism

A memory game played with two packs of cards, named for the Pelman Institute in London, founded to train the memory.

## Pope Joan

A complicated card game, resembling Michigan, named for the fictitious heroine of the satirical romance *Pope Joan* by Greek novelist E. Roidis (1835–1904).

## Slobberhannes (German: "Sloppy Johnny")

A variation of hearts in which the object is to avoid taking the first and last tricks, named for some unknown (and presumably untidy) John.

## Yarborough

A hand in bridge or whist that has no card higher than a nine, named for Charles Anderson Worsley, second earl of Yarborough, who bet 1000–1 against this kind of hand coming up—and lost.

# AMUSEMENT PARKS . . .

## Annie Oakley

A free ticket or pass of admittance, well punched by ticket takers,

named for the famed female sharpshooter who used to shoot out the
pips on a playing card as part of her act.

## catherine wheel

A spinning fireworks that sends out sparks of colored fire, named for
Saint Catherine of Alexandria, who was purportedly martyred on a
spiked wheel in 307 A.D. Actually scholars are skeptical that Catherine
existed at all, but she was widely venerated during the Middle Ages, and
because of the stories surrounding her, any device in the shape of a
spiked wheel is called a catherine wheel.

## Ferris wheel

An amusement-park device consisting of a large wheel with seats or
cars suspended from it at intervals, which revolves, carrying the
passengers around and around, named for George Washington Ferris
(1859–1896), who invented it.

Sponsors of the 1893 World's Columbian Exhibition in Chicago
wanted to build a structure that would rival the famed Eiffel Tower in
Paris, erected for an exhibition there in 1889, and the original Ferris
wheel was the result. It stood 250 feet high and carried thirty-six cars,
each capable of holding forty passengers.

In a way, the sponsors succeeded beyond their imaginings, for there is
only one Eiffel Tower, but there are many thousands of Ferris wheels,
entertainment devices delighted in by children and adults alike.

## Kewpie doll

A trademark for a variety of cheap (originally celluloid) baby dolls
with a topknot of hair through which a ribbon can be looped, named for
Cupid, the god of love, often depicted as a chubby baby.

## teddy bear

A stuffed toy bear with movable arms and legs, usually of plush,
named for President Theodore Roosevelt (1858–1919), who was depicted in a 1902 cartoon as sparing the life of a bear cub.

The cartoon was based on a real-life incident, in which Roosevelt, out hunting, saw a bear cub saunter across his path. He lowered his rifle and said to his companion, "I'll hold my fire for anything that cute." Washington *Star* cartoonist Clifford Berryman heard the story and drew the cartoon, and when the manufacturer saw it, he requested permission of the President to use his nickname, and it was granted.

There have been few toys so universally popular and so loved to death by their child owners as the teddy bear.

# THEATER, FILMS, AND TELEVISION . . .

## chautauqua

Popular entertainment combined with "uplifting" lectures and concerts, named for the Chautauqua Movement, founded at Lake Chautauqua, New York, in 1874. Originally it was a Sunday school for summer visitors to the lake, but in time it mushroomed into traveling shows that offered a wide variety of interesting and entertaining performances.

## lyceum

A place for holding public lectures or discussions, named for the Lyceum outside Athens where the philosopher Aristotle taught. The school in turn took its name from a nearby temple dedicated to Apollo Lyceus ("wolf-slaying Apollo").

## sardoodledom

Staginess, artificial contrivances of plot and character, named for Victorien Sardou (1831–1908), whose plays reflected this kind of technique—at least in the eyes of critic George Bernard Shaw, who coined the term.

## thespian

High-flown term for an actor, named for Thespis, Greek poet of the sixth century B.C. Thespis is credited with developing the individual actor's role in drama, particularly tragedy. Before his time, all lines and actions were performed by choruses.

## vaudeville

Variety entertainment in specialized acts, including singing, dancing, animal acts, juggling, comedy skits, and so on, named ultimately for the *vau-de-Vire* (French: "valley of the Vire") in Normandy.

It was in this region that the art of composing satirical songs in a particular mode was first invented, named "the art of the Vire Valley" because its performers were forbidden by law to engage in true drama and hence could not call themselves actors. Legitimized in the late-nineteenth century, vaudeville (as the name had now become) was the people's entertainment of the day, and as such the name crossed the Atlantic. Thus what was called a music hall in England became a vaudeville theater in the United States.

## yagi

A directional shortwave antenna, named for Hidetsugu Yagi (b. 1886), the Japanese engineer who invented it.

Television got its start in 1883, when Paul Nipkow invented a scanning device. The British began regular television broadcasts in 1937, and the first official network to broadcast in the United States was NBC on February 1, 1940.

# Part 5

SOCIETY'S NEEDS

# · 11 ·

# Economics And
# Government –
# A Social Contract

In our crowded planet, people have found it necessary to regulate their lives, and thus economics and government have come into being. Between them they have produced a bumper crop of useful words.

## ECONOMICS

## MEDIUMS OF EXCHANGE . . .

### balboa

Panama's principal monetary unit, named in honor of Vasco Nuñez de Balboa (1475–1519), first European to cross the Isthmus and discover the Pacific Ocean.

### bolivar

Venezuela's chief monetary unit, named for the Liberator, Simón Bolivar (1783–1830). The country of Bolivia was also named for this South American hero.

### colon

Basic monetary unit of El Salvador and Costa Rica, named in honor of Christopher Columbus (1451–1506), who is known in Spanish as Cristóbal Colón.

## cordoba

Nicaragua's main monetary unit, named for the Spanish explorer of Nicaragua, Francisco de Córdoba (1475–1526).

## dollar

The basic monetary unit of the United States, Hong Kong, Liberia, Ethiopia, Malaysia, and Trinidad and Tobago, named for Joachimsthal ("Joachim valley"), a silver-mining town in Bohemia (now Jáchymov, Czechoslovakia).

In 1519 the people of the town struck a silver coin carrying the likeness of Saint Joachim, father of the Virgin Mary, and called it a *Joachimsthaler*. From *thaler* comes our word "dollar," which from the sixteenth century on became a common term for any silver coin. The Spanish peso, or piece-of-eight, was known to the American colonists as a Spanish dollar.

Therefore it was natural, when it came time for the newly independent United States to select a name for its basic monetary unit, for the government to pick the familiar "dollar."

## franc

The basic monetary unit of many countries—France, Belgium, Switzerland, and a number of African nations—named for the imprint on the original 1360 franc, *Francorum Rex*, "King of the Franks."

## guinea

A gold coin of Great Britain worth twenty-one shillings, minted from 1663 to 1813, named guinea because it was supposed to have been made from gold mined along the Guinea coast of Africa.

## haler

A small Czechoslovakian coin, named for the German town of Hall in Swabia, West Germany, where halers (or hellers) were first minted.

## lempira

Honduras' basic monetary unit, named in honor of a valiant Indian chief who resisted Spanish conquest.

## leone

The basic monetary unit of the African republic of Sierra Leone, named after itself.

## pahlavi

A gold coin of Iran, first issued in 1927 and named for the then ruler, Reza Shah Pahlavi (1877-1944). His son Mohammed Reza Pahlavi, succeeded him on his death and held power in Iran until deposed in the fall of 1978.

## tontine

A type of insurance lottery in which a group of participants (often children) contribute a certain amount of money and the full sum goes to the last surviving member, named for Lorenzo Tonti (1635–1690), an Italian banker in Paris, who advised Louis XIV to incorporate such a device in 1689.

# WORKERS AND THEIR TOOLS . . .

## abigail

A lady's maid, named for the fictional Abigail in Beaumont and Fletcher's 1616 play *The Scornful Lady.*

## bobby

An English term for a policeman, named for Sir Robert Peel, who as Home Secretary in Wellington's Cabinet was responsible for the formation and organization of London's famed Metropolitan Police.

The English so dreaded turning themselves into a police state that for many decades Londoners put up with extreme lawlessness rather than accept a professional force of trained policeman. When it was first introduced in 1829, the bobbies walked the streets without guns or other weapons except a truncheon and have continued unarmed to this day.

## boniface

A hotel or restaurant owner, named for the fictional Boniface in George Farquhar's 1707 comedy *The Beaux' Stratagem*.

## Charley

A night watchman, named for Charles I, who beefed up the watch in London in the 1640's.

## coolie

A menial or unskilled laborer, especially one imported from the Far East to work at subsistence wages, possibly named for the Kuli tribe of Gujarat, an area in western India comprising parts of several modern states.

## derrick

Any kind of hoisting apparatus equipped with rope tackle, named for a seventeenth-century English hangman named Derrick who had his own specially devised equipment.

## drägermen

Miners trained in underground rescue operations, named for Alexander B. Dräger, a German scientist who invented a special type of oxygen inhalator and gas mask used in this work.

## gandy dancer

Member of a section gang, working to repair or lay railroad track, named for the Gandy Manufacturing Company of Chicago, which made tools for this work.

## Ganymede

A youthful bartender, named for the mythical Ganymede, a handsome Trojan boy who was taken to Olympus by Zeus to serve as cupbearer to the gods.

## Okie

A migrant farm worker, named for the State of Oklahoma, where many farms were wiped out during the Dust Bowl years, forcing their owners to sell out and move.

## peavey

A logger's tool made with a sharp metal point and a hook, named for its American inventer, Joseph Peavey. A peavey was an indispensable tool for a log drive, especially when the floating logs got wedged into a jam and had to be picked apart piece by piece—a dangerous assignment calling for a high degree of skill and dexterity.

## Stakhanovite

A worker in a Soviet factory who maintains a consistently high output, named for Aleksei G. Stakhanov, a mineworker who set a record on the night of August 30–31, 1935, by mining 102 tons of coal in one shift—fourteen times the usual rate. Stalin honored Stakhanov for this feat and used it as an example for workers in other occupations to emulate.

# POLITICAL BELIEFS AND TECHNIQUES . . .

## Fabianism

A doctrine of bringing about reform and change by slow, careful, evolutionary means rather than by violent overthrow, named for the Roman general Quintus Fabius Maximus Verrucosus, called Cunctator ("the Delayer"), because of his tactics against Hannibal in the Second Punic War.

Fabius avoided direct battles, exhausted his opponent with harassment and forced marches, and struck at his perimeter and lines of communication. In the end Hannibal retired, unvictorious. George Washington, who employed similar wait-and-see tactics in the Revolutionary War, is often called the American Fabius.

The British Fabian Society was founded in 1884 to bring about social progress by well-planned degrees.

## fourierism

A theory that advocated organizing society into small autonomous communal groups, named for Charles Fourier (1772–1837), French social scientist. His ideas influenced Karl Marx and were later reflected in the Israeli kibbutzim and to some extent in American hippie communes.

## Gandhism

A political theory—called *satyagraha* in India—which relies on truth and expects to achieve its goals by means of tolerance, goodwill, and passive resistance to evil, named for the great Indian leader who brought the movement to life, Mohandas K. Gandhi (1869–1948).

Gandhi—named Mahatma, "Great Soul"—had enormous influence among native leaders seeking to liberate their peoples from colonialism, and was in particular the inspiration for the America black civil-rights leader, Dr. Martin Luther King, Jr.

# hobbism

The belief that the various interests of society are in natural conflict with one another and must be controlled by a strong central government, particularly a monarchical one, named for its original promulgator, the English philosopher Thomas Hobbes (1588–1679).

# McCarthyism

Attack on one's political opponents by unsubstantiated allegations of misconduct, innuendo, and publicity, named for Senator Joseph R. McCarthy of Wisconsin (1909–1957), who attained international fame (or perhaps infamy) by irresponsible attacks on various employees of the federal government, whom he charged with Communist associations.

# malthusianism

A belief that, unless checked by artificial means or some natural disaster, population will inevitably outstrip food production, named for Thomas Malthus (1766–1834), who proposed this theory in *An Essay on the Principle of Population* (1798).

# Maoism

Marxism as adapted for the Chinese experience, named for the Chinese Communist leader Mao Tse-tung (1893–1976).

# Marxism

A belief that history is based on class struggle and that ultimately the workers (the oppressed class) will overthrow the bourgeois capitalists and establish the dictatorship of the proletariat, named for its principal enunciator Karl Marx (1818–1883). Marx and his friend and interpreter Friedrich Engels (1820–1895) stated their basic premise in the 1848 booklet, *The Communist Manifesto*.

## Saint-Simonianism

A form of socialism in which all property is owned by the state and workers are paid according to the amount and quality of their work, named for the French philosopher Claude Henri de Rouvroy (1760–1825), count of Saint Simon, who engineered the basic idea.

# POLITICS . . .

## Australian ballot

A ballot printed at government (not party) expense with the names of the candidates and distributed only at the polls, named "Australian" because it was first used there in the 1850's.

An Australian ballot may be either a Massachusetts ballot (one in which the candidates are listed in alphabetical order, with their party affiliations, under the name of the office they are seeking), the office-block ballot (same as the Massachusetts except that party affiliations are missing), or the Indiana ballot (one in which the names of the candidates are listed in columns under their party affiliations, usually with the party emblem at the top).

The word "ballot" itself is from the Italian word *ballotta,* "little ball," and probably refers back to Periclean Athens, where people voted by dropping pebbles into jars.

In colonial America, corn kernel or beans were dropped into voting boxes, and when fraternal societies vote whether or not to admit a new member, a white ball indicates acceptance, whereas to be "blackballed" is to be denied membership. Paper ballots may have made their first appearance in America in 1629 at Salem, Massachusetts, church meeting.

## balkanize

To divide an area into small divisions in order to weaken it, named for the Balkan Peninsula, historically the home of petty, ineffectual, and quarreling states.

## Big Brother

An omnipresent, spying, totalitarian government, named for the fictional Big Brother in George Orwell's horror novel *1984.*

## boycott

An organized or semiorganized act of ostracism, exerted in order to attain some economic or political end, named for Captain Charles Cunningham Boycott (1832–1897), Irish land agent.

In 1880, when Captain Boycott, working for the earl of Erne, refused to lower certain rents, the Irish Land League organized against him. They prevented laborers from working on the estate, stopped his mail deliveries, cut off his food supplies, damaged his property, and refused to talk to him. In the end, it took a force of nine hundred soldiers to rescue the captain.

The most famous boycott in recent American history was probably that of the black population of Montgomery, Alabama, against a local bus company in protest against segregated seating. Led by Dr. Martin Luther King, Jr., a local Baptist minister, fifty thousand Negroes walked to work, formed private car pools, and hitchhiked rather than use the public transportation, and at the end of a year economic pressures forced the company to yield.

## Egeria

A female adviser to statesmen, usually unofficial, named for the nymph Egeria, who instructed Numa Pompilius (715–673 B.C.) in proper forms of public worship in early Rome.

## gerrymander

To redraw the boundaries of a political district in order to give an electoral advantage to a particular party or group, named for Massachusetts governor Elbridge Gerry (1744–1814).

In 1812 Governor Gerry allowed a state-senate district to be redrawn to ensure that the Democratic-Republican (Jeffersonian) Party would control that seat and thus the entire legislative body. The resulting shape of the district was so peculiar that it inspired a political cartoon, depicting it in the shape of a salamander and labeled "Gerry-mander."

## Pooh-Bah

A self-important public figure, especially one who holds more than one office simultaneously, named for the pompous character in Gilbert and Sullivan's comic opera *The Mikado*. When Ko-Ko, a lowly tailor, was appointed Lord High Executioner by the town of Titipoo, the rest of its haughty officials resigned in a huff, and Pooh-Bah took over their offices—and salaries—becoming Lord-High-Everything-Else.

## roorback

A false story devised to harm a political opponent (the opposite of a whitewash), named for the fictional Baron von Roorback, imaginary author of a nonexistent book, *Roorback's Tour Through the Western and Southern States*.

In 1844, the Ithaca, New York, *Chronicle* published a libelous story about Presidential candidate James K. Polk and, when challenged, claimed they had got it from the above "book."

# Part 6

# THE PEOPLE OF THE WORLD: A HISTORY OF CONTRASTS

# · 12 ·

# Symbols of Diversity: Ethnic and Religious Groups

Before the days of rapid transportation and instantaneous communication, the world was a very large place, separated by vast oceans, high mountains, and unsettled wilderness. These geographical barriers made it possible for civilizations to develop in isolated pockets, each with its own individual ways of living, its own ethnic blood lines. The result was the delightful diversity of humankind we know today.

## NATIONALITIES AND ETHNIC GROUPS . . .

### American

A native-born or naturalized resident of North or South America, particularly of the United States, named for the Florentine businessman and navigator Amerigo Vespucci (1454–1512).

Vespucci took part in several early voyages to the New World and is thought to have been among the first to set foot on the mainland of South America. He made some maps of the regions and wrote an account of his adventures, which was published in 1507 by a German geographer named Martin Waldseemüller, and it was Waldseemüller who suggested that the land be named America after the Latin form of Amerigo, *Americus*.

### Brother Jonathan

An American, in particular a New Englander, named for Jonathan Trumbull (1710–1785), governor of Connecticut during the Revolution.

Trumbull, a vigorous supporter of the cause of independence, was specially active in obtaining supplies for Washington's army, and whenever the pinch set it, Washington was wont to say, "We must consult Brother Jonathan."

The term was once used much as "Yankee" is today—by the British to refer to an American, by a Southerner to refer to a Northerner, and by a Northerner to refer to a New Englander.

## Caucasian

A member of the white race, named for the Caucasus Mountains in the Soviet Union, where whites were supposed to have originated.

In 1795, German anthropologist Johann Blumenbach divided the peoples of mankind into five races: Mongolian, Ethiopian (black), American (Indian), Malayan, and Caucasian.

## Chicano

A Mexican-American, named probably from an early pronunciation of "Mexican." In Spanish x is given a guttural quality, which often transliterates into English as ch.

## Gibson girl

An idealized American young woman, named for artist Charles Dana Gibson (1867–1944), who drew pictures of such girls for illustrations in turn-of-the-century magazines. Typically, the Gibson girl wears a high pompadour, a slender skirt, and a shirtwaist blouse and appears both athletic and dignified.

## gypsy

Anyone who lives a roaming or unsettled life, named for the Gypsies of Europe, famed for their itinerance and their adherence to certain specialized trades, notably, horse training and trading, fortune-telling, and playing dance music.

The Gypsies themselves are named (at least in English) for Egypt, which is where they were thought to originate. Actually they migrated to Europe in the fourteenth century from northwest India and Persia.

## John Bull

The British nation personified, named for the fictional John Bull in John Arbuthnot's satirical *The History of John Bull* (1712). John Bull is usually depicted as a bluff, hearty, red-cheeked country squire, dressed in garments popular in the early nineteenth century.

## Milesian

An Irishman, particularly as a representative of the ancient Celtic race, named for Milesius, a mythical Spanish king, who is said to have conquered Ireland in 1300 B.C. and is considered a forebear of the Irish people.

## Semite

In the broad sense, anyone who speaks one of the Semitic languages (Arabic, Hebrew, Babylonian, Assyrian, Phoenician, etc.), but in the narrow sense, a Jew, named for Shem, son of Noah, from whom both Jews and Arabs are supposedly descended.

In Bible terms, the blacks of Africa are considered to be the descendants of Ham and the whites of Europe the descendants of Japheth, Noah's other two sons.

## Sephardim

One of the two principal divisions of Jews (the other is Ashkenazim), inhabiting chiefly the far western reaches of Europe, named for a region supposedly in northern Asia Minor named Sepharad. (The reference in Obadiah 20 is obscure.)

After the Temple was destroyed in 586 B.C., the Jews dispersed, one group held captive for a while in Sepharad. This group later migrated to Spain and Portugal, which they called Sepharad after their place of captivity. From Iberia, the Sephardim drifted to other regions, notably to the Netherlands, England, and America.

The Ashkenazim settled originally in Germany (*Ashk'naz* is Hebrew for Germany), then spread gradually eastward throughout Poland, Russia, and the Baltic countries. They constitute more than 80 percent of world Jewry and speak Yiddish, a dialect of German written in Hebrew characters.

## Uncle Sam

The personification of the United States named for Samuel Wilson (1766–1854), a meat packer of Troy, New York. During the War of 1812, Wilson contracted to supply the government with meat for its troops, and when friends asked him what the "U.S." stamped on the casks meant, he jokingly replied that they stood for his own nickname: "Uncle Sam."

Uncle Sam is usually depicted as a lean, white-haired, goateed man, dressed in the costume of the 1830's. In 1961 Congress passed a special resolution, recognizing him as America's symbol.

## WASP

An acronym, formed from the initial letters of "White Anglo-Saxon Protestant," for Americans of predominantly British stock and Protestant religion. The term is usually employed pejoratively, implying that the person so named occupies an ethnically privileged position.

# RELIGOUS TERMS . . .

## Amish

Member of a strict Protestant religious sect, an offshoot of the Mennonites, named for its founder, Jacob Ammen, a seventeenth-century Swiss Mennonite bishop.

The Amish, virtually all of whom now reside in North America, live chiefly by farming, dressing in dark, conservative clothes, avoiding mechanical contrivances including cars, and wearing beards. They have maintained their identity and strong religious unity chiefly by avoiding contact with outside groups, in some cases even resisting the compulsory-education laws.

## Arminianism

A doctrine that denied the Calvinist belief in absolute predestination and held that all men were capable of salvation, named for its promulgator Jacobus Arminius (1560–1609), a Dutch theologian.

## Benedictine

Members of the Benedictine order of religious—priests, nuns, and lay brothers—the oldest of all Roman Catholic orders, named for its founder, Saint Benedict of Nursia (480–547).

Benedict is regarded as the founder of monasticism as it was known in medieval Europe, basing his rule on a careful division of the canonical day into hours for work, study, prayer, meditation, and recitation of the Divine Office. The site of his original foundation, the monastery of Monte Cassino near Rome, is considered by Italians a national monument, and although repeatedly ravaged throughout the ages (most recently by Allied bombing in World War II), it still stands on its hilltop.

## Buddhism

The teachings of an Asiatic religion that the sufferings of life can be escaped by mental and moral effort, named for its founder Gautama Buddha (566–486 B.C.).

In his early years, Gautama Siddhartha, son of a wealthy ruler of a Himalayan kingdom, found his life boring and wasteful. He went seeking enlightenment, and one day, in the village of Buddh Gaya, sitting under a pipal tree (later called the sacred Bo tree), he found the new way of life he had been seeking. He spent the next forty-five years traveling up and down the Ganges Valley, teaching his philosophy. He is known now as Buddha, "the Enlightened One."

Buddhism, which has spread all over Asia from Ceylon to Japan, nevertheless has fewer adherents than one would expect—some 261 million, compared to 518 million Hindus, 576 million Muslims, and 984 million Christians.

## Calvinism

The theological teachings of a branch of Protestant Christianity, which holds among other tenets that God alone predetermines who is saved and who is not, named for its promulgator John Calvin (1509–1564). Born in Noyon, Picardy (now Oise), France, he was banished to Switzerland at the age of twenty-four. He eventually established Geneva as the seat of the Reformed Church.

## Carthusianism

A member of the Carthusian order of religious, named for a corrupted Latin form of the site of its mother house, La Grande Chartreuse, Isère, France. (See *chartreuse*.)

## Christianity

The doctrines taught by Jesus Christ (d. A.D. 29) and named for him. "Christ" is from the Greek work *christos,* "the Anointed One," which in turn is translation of the Hebrew *Messiah.*

## Cistercian

Member of the Cistercian order of religious, named for the town of Cistercium (now Cîteaux) near Dijon, Côtes d'Or, France, where its first monastery was founded. The Cistercians, famed for the austerity of their life, are now divided into two groups, the Cistercians proper and the Trappists (named for their first monastery, founded at La Trappe in Normandy).

## Dominican

A member of the Order of Preaching Friars, named for its founder, Saint Dominic (1170–1221). The Dominicans were known in medieval England as Blackfriars, from the color of their cloaks.

Four Dominicans became popes, and numerous others were in the front rank of theological learning and philosophy. In time, largely because of their status as intellectuals, Dominicans came to dominate the Inquisition, which might have distressed their founder exceedingly, for Dominic was a man of deep compassion for human suffering.

Today Dominicans live, work, preach, and teach all over the world.

## Dorcas Society

A women's volunteer church group or sewing circle, formed to make clothes for the poor, named for the charitable woman Dorcas, whom the Apostle Peter raised from the dead:

> Now there was at Joppa a certain disciple named Tabitha, which by interpretation is called Dorcas: this woman was full of good works and almsdeeds which she did. . . . Peter . . . kneeled down, and prayed; and turning him to the body said, Tabitha, arise. And she opened her eyes. . . . (Acts 9:36–40)

## Druze

Member of a small religious sect, an offshoot of Islam, whose members (dwelling chiefly in the mountains of Lebanon and Syria) hold beliefs drawn from Muhammadanism, Christianity, and Judaism, named for its principal preacher, Muhammad-ibn-Ismail al-Daraziy. The actual founder of the religion was the eleventh-century caliph Hakim.

## Franciscan

A member of the Order of Friars Minor, named for its founder, Saint Francis of Assisi (1182–1226), who devoted his life to preaching to the poor.

The Franciscans, known in medieval England as Grey Friars from the color of their somber habit, comprise three distinct orders: friars proper, Poor Clares (sisters), and Tertiaries—laymen and diocesan clergy who have devoted their lives to penance.

## Hinduism

The dominant religion of India, comprising a complicated set of religious and social beliefs, based on a rigid system of caste, named for the Persian word for India.

## Huguenot

A French Calvinist of the sixteenth and seventeenth centuries, named for Besançon Hugues, a sixteenth-century Genevan who in 1535 led a movement of his fellow Calvinists to prevent the annexation of their territory by the Catholic duke of Savoy.

An alternate explanation of the name is that the first French Protestants held their nightly meetings at the gate of Roi-Hugon in Tours, Indre-et-Loire, France.

## Jesuit

Member of an order of Roman Catholic priests, whose common name is derived from the organization's formal one: the Society of Jesus.

The society was founded in 1534 by Saint Ignatius Loyola (1491–1556) as a means of combating Protestantism with argument and persuasion. His first recruit for the new order was Saint Francis Xavier (1506–1552), a fellow Basque. The two died within four years of one another and were canonized the same year.

## Jew

A member of the world's first monotheistic religion, whose name derives from Judah, the fourth son of Jacob.

And she [Leah] conceived again, and bare a son; and she said, Now will I praise the Lord: therefore she called his name Judah. . . . (Genesis 29:35)

## Lutheranism

The theological teachings of the oldest branch of Protestant Christianity, named for its founder, Martin Luther (1483–1546). An Augustinian friar and ordained priest, Luther became disgusted with the excesses and venalities common to the Church of his day, and in 1517 he wrote out a public protest against them—the famed Ninety-Five Theses—and nailed it to the church door in Wittenberg, East Germany, the city where he was teaching. This is usually regarded as the single act that opened the Protestant Reformation.

Luther later married a former nun, translated the Scriptures from Latin into his native German, and founded the Evangelical Church.

## Magen David ("The Shield of David")

Two intersecting equilateral triangles forming a six-pointed star, the symbol of Judaism, named for David, king of Israel and Judah.

The Magen David, also called the Star of David, is to Jews what the cross is to Christians and appears in blue, against a white field, on the Israeli flag.

## Manichaeism

A religion of the early Christian era, containing many elements similar to Christianity and others apparently derived from Zoroastrianism, named for its founder, the Persian sage Manes (216–276).

In order to divorce the spirit (allied with light and goodness) from the body (allied with darkness and evil), the Manichaean was urged to practice asceticism and avoid procreation.

## maumet

A false god or idol, named for Muhammad, the Prophet and founder of Islam. In the Middle Ages Christians believed that Muslims worshiped and prayed to images of Muhammed. Actually, of course, Islam is as austere as Judaism in banning the use of paintings and statuary in its houses of religion.

## Mennonite

Member of a small Protestant sect, famed for the plainness of its dress and its aloofness from the state, named for its founder Menno Simons (1492–1559), a Frisian religious reformer.

Most Mennonites now reside in the United States and Canada and are relatively indistinguishable in dress and manner from their neighbors. In this they differ sharply from their daughter religionists, the Amish.

## Millerite

A believer in the doctrines of millerism, named for its founder William Miller (1782–1849), a farmer who predicted that the world would end on October 22, 1844. On that day, thousands of Millerites left their homes and jobs, donned ascension robes, and waited on mountaintops or in cemeteries for the world to end.

## Mormon

A member of the Church of Jesus Christ of Latter-Day Saints, named Mormon from the *Book of Mormon,* one of the Church's Scriptural authorities. The book in turn takes its name from the prophet Mormon, believed by Mormons to be the author.

The founder of the Church, Joseph Smith (1805–1844), claimed to have discovered a series of gold tablets containing the *Book of Mormon,* written in "reformed Egyptian," which he translated into English. They tell of migrations of Hebrews to the New World in ancient times, where they settled and became the Indians.

## Muhammadanism

The religion of Islam ("Submission to the Will of God"), named for its Prophet and founder, Muhammad (570–632).

Left an orphan, Muhammad was raised by an uncle, became a camel driver and shepherd, then married a rich widow, whose wealth gave him the leisure to meditate on the condition of his Arab peoples, to envision a frame of beliefs, and to receive the call to preach to them a new religion.

Even before the Prophet's death, Islam had spread through the Arabian peninsula. Within a century, it reigned supreme from Spain across North Africa and into India.

## Parsiism

A Zoroastrian of India, whence members of this religious group fled in the seventh century to escape Muslim persecution in their homeland, named for the Old Persian word for Persia.

## Rosicrucian

Member of an occult organization which claims to hold special esoteric knowledge, named for its purported fifteenth-century founder, Christian Rosenkreutz (German: "Rosy Cross"). Modern-day members of the *Fraternitas Rosae Crucis* (Latin: "Brotherhood of the Rosy Cross") study religious mysticism and attempt to apply it to contemporary problems.

## Salesian

Member of an order of religious founded in the nineteenth century by Saint John Bosco (1815–1888) and named for an earlier saint, Francis de Sales (1567–1622).

Bosco devoted his life to the plight of homeless boys, setting up centers throughout Turin, Italy, to house, feed, and teach them trades.

## Satanism

The worship of the devil, derived from Shatan, the Old Testament word for "adversary." Shatan was allowed to inflict great torment on Job to see if he could shatter his loyalty to God.

The word "devil" is from the Greek *diabolos*—"slanderer."

## Thomism

The theological system of thought that dominated the late Middle Ages, named for Saint Thomas Aquinas (1225–1274), who promulgated it.

## Ursuline

Member of an order of sisters, founded in the sixteenth century to educate girls, named for the legendary Saint Ursula.

According to the story, Ursula, daughter of an ancient British king, was returning from a pilgrimage to Rome when at Cologne she encountered a band of pagan Huns, who slaughtered her and her followers. The latter were originally listed as ten, but in retelling, the eleven girls became expanded to eleven thousand virgins.

## Waldenses

The followers of a medieval religion (regarded as heretical by the Church of Rome) similar to Manichaeism, named for its founder Peter Waldo (1140–1218). Persecuted bitterly by the Church, the Waldenses managed to survive by secrecy and a retreat into the mountains of the Piedmont in Italy, and in the sixteenth century they became Calvinists.

## Zoroastrianism

A religion of ancient, pre-Islamic Persia, in which good and light are represented by the god Ahura Mazda and evil and darkness by the devil Ahriman, named for its founder, Zoroaster (or Zarathustra).

# A SAMPLING OF NATIONAL SPECIALTIES . . .

Numerous words are preceded by adjectives derived from the names of many nations, often describing something found in that particular country. Only the largest national categories are included here.

## Australian:

anteater, badger, ballot, banyon, baobab, bean tree, bear, beech, beech cherry, black wood, bluebell, brake, cat, cattle dog, cherry,

cockroach, cranberry, crawl, currant, desert kumquat, English, football, gourd, grass tree, gum, heath, heeler, honeysuckle, ironbark,
laurel, lilac, magpie, mahogany, millet, nettle tree, nut, oak, oat,
opossum, pea, pine, pirpiri, pitcher plant, plague locust, poker, snail,
rosewood, salmon, saltbush, sarsaparilla, sassafras, sea holly, sham-
rock, sugar tree, swamp oak, tamarind, teak, terrier, turpentine tree,
walnut, water lily, water rat, willow, X-disease.

## Dutch:

auction (start high, go down), backgammon, bargain (a deal made
while drinking), barn, bath, beech, belted (a variety of milk cow), blue,
bob or cut (short haircut with bangs), brass, bulb, cap (woman's hat),
cheese, clinker (a kind of brick), clover, colonial, courage (false bravery
derived from alcohol, etc.), curse (a daisy), door (has a separate top and
bottom), elm, engine, flax, foot (a hoof-shaped furniture leg), frill
(canary), gabled, grass, hoe (both sides of garden hoe are sharpened),
iris, lap (way to place roof shingles), lottery (winners are in categories),
lunch (cold cuts and cheeses), metal (imitation gold leaf), myrtle,
orange, oven, pen, pink, process, rabbit, roll (airplane turn), rose (a
diamond cut), scarlet, settle (wooden bench), straight (to skip straight),
treat (pay your own way), 200 (bowling score of strikes and spares),
uncle (a blunt reprimander), wife (bolster), woodbine.
*Dutchman:* a method of hiding poor work
*Dutchman's:* breeches (a flower), log (a way to calculate boat speed),
pipe (a vine).
*Dutch:* disfavor, trouble. To dutch: figure bets wrong.

## English:

basement (an above-ground, separate entrance to an apartment),
billiards (six pockets), bluebell, bluegrass, bond (a method of laying
brick), breakfast tea (black tea), bulldog, camomile, chop (lamb chop
that is boned out with a kidney put in), corn (wheat), cowslip, daisy,
disease (rickets), elm, equatorial (a telescope), finish (smooth paper
finish), flute, foot (a sole on hosiery with a seam on each side of it),
foxhound, gooseberry, grain aphid, grass, green, guitar, harvest
(wheat), hawthorn, hay, herring, holly, horn, iris, ivy, last (a shoe last),
laurel, loose (an archery release), maidenhair, man's knot (a fisherman's knot), maple, muffin, oak, ocher, opera (a ballad opera), pea,

pink, plantain, pool, primrose, rabbit, red, Rite (a Masonic ceremony), rubin, ryegrass, saddle (has long side bars and no horn), setter, shepherd, snipe, sole, sonnet, sparrow, springer, system (a way to spin wool into yarn), thistle, toy Spaniel, tubol, vermilion, violet, wallflower, walnut, wheat, white, yew.

## French:

anemone, arch, bean, beaver (rabbit fur made to look like beaver), bed (head and foot have scrolls), beige, berry, blue, boston (a card game), bowline, bracket foot, bread, brier, bulldog, canna, chalk (dry-cleaning grease remover), chestnut, Chippendale, chop (meat trimmed at end of rib chop), cleaner (dry cleaner), clover, cocklebur, column, combing wool, cooking, cuff (cuff links hold doubled shirt cuffs), curve, cut (meat cut a certain way—in strips, etc.), disease (syphilis), door (glass panels), doughnut (cream-puff dough, deep-fat fried), drain, dressing (oil-and-vinegar salad dressing), drip (drip coffee), endive, fake (a way to coil a rope), fold (fold reading material), folio (light writing paper), foot (hosiery seam runs from sole to back of leg), fried potato, fry (browned in deep fat), fryer (a deep pan with a wire basket), gray, green, grunt (a fish), handwork (fancy laundry hand-done service), harp (a harmonica), -headed (material with pinch pleats), heel (high-curved woman's shoe), hem (method of seaming), honeysuckle, hood (a woman's headdress), horn, ice cream (cream and egg yolks are used to make this frozen yellow custard), kid (a special method for tanning kidskin), kiss (a deep kiss), knot (a fancy stitch), lavender, leave (a fast departure), leg, letter (a condom), lug, marigold, molt, morocco, mulberry, nude (a light-brown color), ocher, order (architecture), partridge, pastry (fancy custard or fruit portions), pea, pink, pitch, plague or pox (syphilis), polish (oil- and shellac-rubbed furniture finish), Provincial (furniture style), reef, roast (coffee that is dark roasted), roll, roof, rose, sage, sash, scarlet, scroll, seam, silver (rabbits with silvery coats), sole, sorrel, spinach, spun, tack, tamarisk, tea, telephone, tip, toast (bread dipped in egg and milk, then fried), toe (a square-tip shoe), trumpet, ultramarine, varnish, vermilion, vermouth, veronese, weed, willow, window, yellow.

## Scotch:

barley, blue, brier, broom, broth (beef or mutton, vegetables and barley), cap, carpet, cart, collie, comb, crocus, deerhound, douche (a douche that can spray hot or cold water), edge (shoe edge), elm, fiddle (an itch), fingering, fir, gale, grain (coarse pebbled leather grain), grass, gray, hands (paddles used to prepare butter), heath, hoppers (hopscotch), marigold, marriage (common-law), mist (dense mist and drizzle), nightingale, pebble (polished quartz), pine, rose, snap, tape, terrier, thistle, topaz, verdict (an indecisive decision), whisky, whist, woodcock (anchovy paste, scrambled eggs on toast), yoke.

To *scotch:* to stamp out, stop.


## Spanish:

bayonet (a plant), billiards, bluebell, bowline, broom (a shrub), brown, buttons (a plant), carnation, cedar, chalk, chestnut, clover, cream, curlew, dagger (a plant), elm, fir, flag (a fish), fly (European blister beetle), foot (clawed foot on furniture), fox, grain (fancy leather-embossed texture), grape, green, grunt (a fish), guitar, heath, heel (a leather-covered wooden heel), bogfish, Inquisition, influenza (widespread, pandemic), iris, jacinth, jasmine, lady (a bonefish), leather, lettuce, licorice, lime, lobster, mackerel, mahogany, Main (South American coast), measles (a grapevine disease), moss, needles, oak, ocher, omelet (eggs, onion, tomato, chopped green pepper and sauce), onion, oxide, oyster, pack (forty playing cards with no eights, nines, or tens), paprika, peanut, pear, pepper, plum tomato, red, rice (tomatoes, green peppers, and onions), rococo, sage, sauce (flour-thickened brown sauce), scroll (a fancy furniture foot scroll), sheep, soldier (speargrass), spoon (a long-handled posthole digger), stopper (a tree), tea, thistle, toothpick (a plant), topaz, trefoil, white, windlass, wine (pigeon blood), yellow.

# · 13 ·

# A Closer World: Transportation

People have always found the need to travel, whether for safety, for finding food, for employment, or for pleasure. They went by foot, on horseback, by automobile, by sea, by air. En route, they have picked up numerous souvenirs to add to our vocabularies.

## WALKING . . .

### Malacca cane

A walking stick of mottled appearance cut from the rattan palm, and named for the province of Malacca in Malaysia, where it is chiefly found.

## CARRIAGES . . .

### Berlin

A four-wheeled vehicle with a separate hooded seat behind, named for the city where it was designed and first used.

### brougham

A light carriage with a closed compartment for two passengers and an open seat for the driver, named for Henry Peter Brougham, Baron

266

Brougham and Vaux (1778–1868), Scots jurist, who designed the original. The front wheels are made small so that the vehicle can execute a sharp turn.


## clarence

A closed carriage seating four with an outside driver's seat, named for Prince William Henry (1765–1837), duke of Clarence and St. Andrews (later King William IV). A clarence is similar to a brougham except that it is larger and the driver sits higher up, to accommodate the front wheels, nearly as large as the back ones.


## Conestoga wagon

A boat-shaped covered wagon for hauling freight, named for the town where it was designed and built, Conestoga, Pennsylvania. Conestogas, drawn by four to six specially bred horses, each equipped with an arch of bells (they were called bell teams), could carry a load of three to six tons.

The Conestoga was used from 1750 to 1850 for hauling furs and trade goods, chiefly between Conestoga and Pennsylvania, but also to points west along the National Road. It was the granddaddy of the famed prairie schooner—a much lighter vehicle.


## fiacre

A hired vehicle, especially the small hackney coaches common to French cities, named for the Hôtel-de-Saint-Fiacre, a seventeenth-century Parisian inn near which cabs lined up to wait for passengers.

Saint Fiacre himself was a seventh-century Irish hermit, who set up a hospice for travelers near Meaux (now Seine-et-Marne), France.


## hansom

A light two-seater carriage, used chiefly as a taxicab, in which the driver sits above and behind the passengers and the reins pass over their heads, named for Joseph A. Hansom (1803–1882), an architect who invented the vehicle.

## landau

A light pleasure carriage with a top that can be partly lowered and partly removed, named for the town of Landau, Bavaria, West Germany, where it was first made.

When the British royal family rides out on an occasion that is formal but not formal enough for the state coach, they usually choose a landau with the top removed.


## phaeton

Any of various light open summer carriages without sides, in which the driver (usually the owner) sits on the same level as the passenger, named for the mythological Phaethon, son of Helios, the Greek sun god, who tried to drive his father's chariot across the sky and nearly succeeded in setting the earth on fire.


## rockaway

A boxy American carriage with a fixed top and open sides, equipped with waterproof curtains, named for the town of Rockaway, New Jersey, where it was manufactured.


## stanhope

A high gig (an open, two-wheeled, one-horse driving vehicle), with a closed back and straight arm rests, named for Fitzboy Stanhope (1787–1864), an English clergyman who ordered the first such carriage.


## surrey

A two-seater pleasure carriage, open-sided, with or without a top, straight-bottomed, named for the county of Surrey, England, where it was first made.

Thanks to the jaunty Rodgers and Hammerstein song, "The Surrey with the Fringe on Top," surreys are among the best-known today of all horse-drawn vehicles.

## tilbury

A two-seater gig, with or without a top, named for a London coachmaker named Tilbury.

## victoria

A two-seater pleasure carriage with a folding top and a high seat for a driver, named for Queen Victoria of England (1819–1901). Many people consider the graceful victoria the most beautiful of all carriages.

# AUTOMOBILES . . .

The automobile has changed the face of America and many other parts of the world. In the United States, at least one of every seven working people has a job that is in some way related to cars, and one in six businesses depend on them. It is estimated that American cars, buses, and trucks traveled at least 1.5 billion miles in 1978, a distance equal to 3 million round trips to the moon.

## berline

A limousine, designed for chauffeur driving, with a sliding glass window between driver's seat and passenger compartment, named for the city of Berlin, probably because it evolved out of the berlin coach.

## Buick

A medium-heavy car built by General Motors and named for David D. Buick (1855–1929), who first developed it. A plumber by trade, Buick was forced out of his own company within four years of his founding it and died a trade-school clerk.

## Cadillac

A heavy passenger vehicle, built by General Motors, named for Sieur Antoine de la Mothe Cadillac, seventeenth-century French colonial administrator and the founder of Detroit.

## Chevrolet

General Motors' lowest-priced passenger car, named for Louis Chevrolet (1879–1941), American car designer, who first built it.

## Chrysler

Chrysler Corporation's heaviest passenger car, named for Walter P. Chrysler (1875–1940), who founded the company.

Chrysler started out as a railroad machinist, then worked his way to the top of the Buick Motor Company, before leaving to found his own firm.

## Ford

Any of several different styles of car produced by the Ford Motor Company, named for its founder and inventor, Henry Ford (1863–1947).

Ford, a machinist like many early auto inventors, founded his own company in 1903 and revolutionized the auto industry by introducing the assembly line, profit sharing, high factory wages, and cheap cars. The famed Model-T, butt of a dozen jokes about Tin Lizzies and the Tin You Love to Touch, first came off the production line in 1908, priced at $825, and was snapped up. By 1927, when the design was abandoned in favor of a more modern one, 15 million Model-T's had been built and sold.

## limousine

A large luxury vehicle, chauffeur-driven and having either an open front seat or one separated from the passenger compartment by a glass window (see *berline*), named for the province of Limousin in central France.

"Limousin" originally meant a cloak or hood, and perhaps it was the "wrapped up" or secluded state of the passenger that led people to apply the term to this rich man's car.

## Oldsmobile

A medium-heavy car manufactured by General Motors and named for Raymond E. Olds, who built the first ones.

## Pontiac

A medium-heavy car manufactured by General Motors and named for the Ottawa chief who led the widest-spread and most nearly successful of all Indian revolts, 1763–1765.

Pontiac's War centered on Fort Detroit, which he planned to take by surprise, but the scheme was betrayed by a girl, and he was forced to settle instead for a months-long siege—uncongenial to Indian temperament. Nevertheless the whites were unable to drive off his followers, and ultimately the siege was only lifted by the arrival of help by way of the Lakes.

## Rolls-Royce

The ultimate luxury in automobiles, manufactured in Manchester, England, and named for the man who invented it (engineer Sir Henry Royce, 1863–1933) and the man who promoted it, (Charles Stewart Rolls, 1877–1910). Rolls, a daredevil pioneer in both auto driving and flying, was the first Englishman to be killed in an airplane.

# TRAINS . . .

## pullman

A railroad sleeping car, named for George Mortimer Pullman (1831–1897). who built the first ones in America. Pullman, a cabinetmaker by training, devised a method of turning daytime seats into nighttime bunks, for use on long-distance and transcontinental trains. In partnership with Andrew Carnegie, he formed the Pullman Palace Car Company to build pullmans and set up the company's own town, Pullman, Illinois, (later incorporated into Chicago) to house workers.

# SHIPS . . .

## hermaphrodite brig

A two-masted vessel carrying a hybrid rig—square on the foremast, fore-and-aft on the main—named for the mythical Hermaphroditus. (See *hermaphrodite.*)

## Indiaman

A large sailing vessel employed in the India trade, especially one flying the burgee of the British East India Company, named for the subcontinent.

## Jacob's ladder

A ladder for climbing the side of a ship, made of rope or chain with rungs of wood or metal, named for the biblical Jacob, who saw a ladder to heaven in a dream:

> And he dreamed, and behold a ladder set up on the earth, and the top of it reached to heaven. . . . (Genesis 28:12)

## Marconi rig

A fore-and-aft rig set on an especially tall mast and a short boom, named for Guglielmo Marconi (1874–1937), Italian physicist who developed wireless telegraphy (radio), probably because the triangular mainsail resembles a radio beacon.

## plimsoll

Load line painted on the hull of a vessel to indicate how deep in the water it may legally sit when fully loaded, named for Samuel Plimsoll (1824–1898), English philanthropist, who was instrumental in obtaining shipping reforms.

Plimsoll, a coal merchant and Member of Parliament, was shocked at the habit of shipowners of callously allowing crews to go to sea in heavily overloaded (and insured) ships. After a long campaign, he induced Parliament to pass the Merchant Shipping Act (1876), which effectively prevented overloading by forcing ships to carry the plimsoll.

## Saint Elmo's fire

A brush discharge of electricity sometimes seen at the masts of ships (or the wingtips of airplanes) in stormy weather, named for Saint Elmo, patron saint of sailors.

Elmo, or Erasmus, was purportedly a second-century bishop of Syria who was martyred, according to the story, by having his entrails wound out of his body on a windlass, and the resemblance of this device to a ship's capstan made sailors adopt him as their own.

## texas

On Mississippi steamboats, a structure on top of the hurricane deck containing the officers' cabins and the pilothouse, named for the then largest state in the Union. It was customary for steamboats to name various cabins after states, so it was natural to name this, the largest one, after Texas.

# AIR TRAVEL . . .

## montgolfier

A fire (hot-air) balloon, named for the Montgolfier brothers, Jacques-Etienne (1745–1799) and Joseph-Michel (1740–1810), who built the first one.

The bag was linen lined with paper, and in order to fill it, they burned straw and wool in an iron brazier in the balloon's basket. On June 5, 1783, it flew for the first time—for ten minutes and one and a half miles—and the following September 19, it flew again, this time carrying the world's first air passengers, a sheep, a duck, and a rooster.

## zeppelin

A dirigible or airship, consisting of a rigid frame, covered with fabric and supported by an internal series of gas bags, named for Graf Ferdinand von Zeppelin, who developed it.

Germany was far ahead of the rest of the world in building airships, employing them during World War I in bombing raids over London. By late 1918, she had perfected a zeppelin that could cross the Atlantic and return without refueling.

The two most famous of all airships were the *Graf Zeppelin,* which in 1929 made an unprecedented flight around the world, and later logged a total of 1,440 transatlantic crossings, and the ill-fated *Hindenburg.* The latter, on the first flight of its second season of commercial ocean crossings, burst into flames at its mooring post in Lakehurst, New Jersey, and killed thirty-six people.

# LUGGAGE . . .

## Boston bag

A purselike traveling bag consisting of a flat, rectangular bottom and sides that taper to a two-handled closure, named for the city of Boston.

## duffel bag

A cylindrical canvas bag for carrying camping or sports gear, named for the town of Duffel, Belgium. The coarse blanketing of which such bags were originally made was manufactured in Duffel.

## Gladstone bag

A traveling bag with flexible sides (usually of leather) over a rigid frame, which opens flat into two equally deep sides, named for William E. Gladstone (1809–1898), four times Prime Minister of Great Britain.

## Saratoga trunk

A large lady's trunk, usually iron bound and with a curved top, named for the famed resort and health spa, Saratoga Springs, New York. A properly made Saratoga trunk was supposedly large enough to carry a month's supply of vacation wardrobe.

# TRAVELING MISCELLANY . . .

## atlas (the book)

A book of maps, named for the mythical Atlas, a Titan who was punished for a rebellion against Zeus by having to carry the sky on his shoulders. In early days, books of maps usually carried a picture of Atlas on their title pages, and in 1595 the son of Gerhardus Mercator issued posthumously his father's famous book, titled *Atlas*.

Mercator (1512–1594), a Flemish cartographer, is famed chiefly for his technique of depicting the round earth on a flat map by showing the lines of longitude parallel instead of converging. This "Mercator projection" distorts the appearance of the earth's land masses, making polar regions appear much larger than they are, but it was useful to navigators in the days before accurate chronometers made it relatively easy to determine longitude.

## Baedeker

A guidebook, particularly to a foreign country, named for Karl Baedeker (1801–1859), German publisher, whose firm produces a series of highly regarded guidebooks of Europe, North America, and Asia.

## cicerone

A sightseer's guide, usually privately hired, named for the famed Roman orator Marcus Tullius Cicero (106–43 B.C.), because such guides are often compulsively talkative.

## lingua franca ("language of the Franks")

A hybrid, usually rudimentary, language, in wide common use over a broad area, which permits persons of different native languages to converse and do business with one another, named for the Frankish language (an admixture of Romance, Greek, and Arabic tongues) used throughout the Mediterranean region during the Middle Ages.

## Magellan

A world traveler, named for Ferdinand Magellan (1480–1521), Portuguese navigator who led the first maritime expedition to circumnavigate the globe. Of the five vessels with which Magellan left Spain, September 20, 1519, only one, the *Victoria,* returned, September 6, 1522. Magellan himself was not aboard, having been killed in the Philippines, but the ship carried a cargo of spices that more than paid for the voyage.

## odyssey

A long journey or campaign, featuring many changes of fortune, named for Homer's epic poem of the ten-year adventures of Odysseus, the Greek hero.

# · 14 ·

# Progress: Products of Inventive Minds

Intelligence, perseverance, and courage are prime ingredients in the makeup of the innovative people who have contributed to the world's progress. It is thus fitting that many of their ideas and devices bear their names.

## INVENTIONS AND MECHANICAL PROCESSES . . .

### Archimedean screw

A device for raising water from a lower level to a higher one, consisting of a tube wound spirally around a central core and capable of being revolved, named for the famed Greek of Syracuse, Archimedes (287–212 B.C.), who invented it.

When one end of the Archimedean screw is dipped slantwise into water and the entire device rotated, water is scooped up and carried higher and higher in the tube until it begins to flow out over the top. It was used for many centuries to lift water from the Nile to irrigate nearby fields.

Archimedes is perhaps most famous for his discovery of the principle of displacement (that a body immersed in water loses weight to the extent of the water displaced). He was attempting to discover a way to determine the purity of the gold in the crown of the ruler of Syracuse, and as he was lying in the public bath, the theory occurred to him. Leaping up, he cried, "*Eureka!* [I found it!]" and hurried home.

## artesian well

A water well, usually drilled deeply into underlying rock, in which hydrostatic pressure forces a strong flow or gush, named for the province of Artois in northern France, where such wells were first dug.

## Bailey bridge

A partly prefabricated bridge, which can be assembled rapidly from interchangeable parts and panel trusses, named for Sir Donald C. Bailey, an English engineer, who invented it in 1941.

## Bakelite

Trade name for a hard synthetic resin plastic, used in the manufacture of pipe mouthpieces, beads, and buttons, named for Leo H. Baekeland (1863–1944), a Belgian-American chemist who invented it in 1907.

## benday

To prepare a piece of artwork for reproduction in a newspaper or magazine by a method that substitutes dots for shaded or tinted areas, named for the inventor of the process, New York printer Benjamin Day (1838–1916).

Day's father, Benjamin Henry Day (1810–1889), founded the New York *Sun* in 1833, America's first successful penny newspaper. His nephew, Clarence Shepherd Day, Jr. (1874–1935), authored a series of essays on his family that ultimately became the perennially popular play *Life with Father*.

## Bessemer process

A low-cost, rapid method of making steel by using a blast of air to rid pig iron of impurities, named for Sir Henry Bessemer (1813–1898), English engineer who invented it.

## Bunsen burner

A small gas flame for use in experimental laboratories, which burns with low illumination but intense heat, named for Robert Wilhelm Bunsen (1811–1899), the German chemist who invented it.

## Cassegrainian telescope

A reflecting telescope in which light is focused through a hole in the primary mirror, named for N. Cassegrain, seventeenth-century French physician, its inventor.

## daguerreotype

An important early process in the development of photography in which an image is produced on a sensitized silver-coated plate and developed by vapor of mercury, named for the inventor of the process, Louis Jacques Mandé Daguerre (1789–1851), French painter.

Daguerre made no attempt to profit from his invention privately but communicated word of it to the French Academy of Sciences (1839). The academy published the process, and to compensate Daguerre, the government awarded him a pension.

## davy lamp

A miner's safety lamp in which metal gauze prevents the illuminating flame from igniting the firedamp pervasive in early mines, named for Sir Humphry Davy, English chemist, who invented it. A brilliant scientist with numerous stunning scientific discoveries to his name, Sir Humphry is nonetheless best remembered for this simple, life-saving device.

## Dewar flask

A forerunner of the thermos bottle, used particularly for the storage of liquefied gases, named for its inventor, Scots chemist Sir James Dewar (1842–1923).

## diesel engine

An internal-combustion engine operating by means of compressed air and fuel injection, named for its inventor, Rudolf Diesel (1858–1913), German mechanical engineer.

## fourdrinier

A papermaking machine that ingests wood pulp and turns out a continuous roll of paper, named for its inventors, the Fourdrinier brothers, Henry (1766–1854) and Sealy (d. 1847).

## Franklin stove

A metal heating stove designed to be placed in the center of a room, named for Benjamin Franklin (1706–1790), who invented it. As with all his inventions (bifocals, lightning rod, smoke-free street lamps), Franklin freely gave away the design, seeking no patent or profit from its use.

Franklin justifiably takes his place among the world's great inventors. In addition to the many small devices he contrived, he founded the American Philosophical Society, laid the foundations for the free circulating libraries we all enjoy, improved colonial postal services, helped found the University of Pennsylvania and the first hospital in the colonies, and, of course, proved that lightning was an electrical discharge. And all this was in addition to his political, diplomatic, and literary achievements.

## galvanized iron

Iron coated by electrical means with zinc to render it rust-resistant, named for Luigi Galvani (1737–1798), Italian physicist, an early experimenter with electricity.

Galvani's name is most commonly associated with the verb "to galvanize," meaning "to rouse up, to inspirit," taken from his technique of causing muscular response in the legs of dead frogs by means of electrical impulses.

## hermetic

An adjective meaning "airtight," named for the Greek name for Thoth, Hermes Trismegistus, the Egyptian god of wisdom, who was supposed to have invented a magic seal that would make vessels airtight.

## klieg light

A very bright carbon-arc light used in filmmaking, named for the German-born Kliegl brothers, John (1869–1959) and Anton (1872–1927), early innovators in the development of motion-picture equipment.

## Leyden jar

An early type of electrical condenser or capacitor, consisting of a glass jar with layers of metal foil inside and out and an insulating stopper, named for the university city of Leiden. Most early experiments with electricity were performed by means of Leyden jars.

## McKay process

An improved technique for manufacturing shoes, named for Gordon McKay (1821–1903), who developed it.

## Morse code

A system for sending messages over the telegraph wires in which dots and dashes in various combinations represent the letters of the alphabet, named for Samuel F. B. Morse (1791–1872), who invented it along with a working form of the magnetic telegraph. On May 24, 1844, Morse sent his famous first message over an experimental line between Baltimore and Washington: "What hath God wrought!"

Perhaps the best known of all Morse-code messages is the distress signal, SOS. This is not an acronym or an abbreviation but simply the easiest and most unmistakable combination to send in code: dot-dot-dot-dash-dash-dash-dot-dot-dot.

## Solvay process

A technique for manufacturing sodium bicarbonate (baking soda), by means of ammonia, salt, limestone, and carbon dioxide, named for its developer, Ernest Solvay (1838–1922), Belgian chemist.

## toledo

A finely tempered sword, named for the city of Toledo, Spain, where sword-making has been a fine art since antiquity.

## vulcanization

The process of treating rubber with sulfur and other chemicals to improve its properties and multiply its uses, named for the Roman god of fire and craftsmanship, Vulcan.

## Welsbach burner

Trademarked name for a gas burner fueled by a mixture of air and gas, which provides light by heating a gauze mantle to incandescence (glowing whiteness), named for its inventor, Baron Carl von Welsbach (1858–1929), an Austrian chemist. Nowadays Welsbach burners are used chiefly on camp lanterns.

# MEASUREMENT UNITS AND DEVICES . . .

## angstrom

A unit of wavelength, named for Ånders Jonas Angström (1814–1874), Swedish physicist who founded the science of spectroscopy. There are two different angstroms—the *absolute angstrom,* measured at 1/10 billionth of a meter, and the *international angstrom,* determined by the wavelength of the red spectrum line of cadmium.

## ampere

A unit of electric current, named for André-Marie Ampère (1775–1836), a French physicist, who is considered the father of electrodynamics.

## Baumé scale

A hydrometer scale for measuring specific gravity, named for Antoine Baumé (1728–1804), a French chemist and pharmacist who invented it.

## Beaufort scale

A scale used to designate the velocity and force of winds, named for Rear Admiral Sir Francis Beaufort (1774–1857), R.N., who devised it.

According to the Beaufort scale, still used by the U.S. Weather Bureau, wind force is indicated by a number between 0 and 17 and a corresponding descriptive word. Force 5, for example, means a wind blowing between 19 and 24 miles per hour and is labeled "fresh breeze," whereas Force 12 means a wind blowing between 73 and 82 miles per hour and is labeled "hurricane."

## Brinell hardness

A scale that designates the relative hardness of different types of metals and alloys, named for Johann August Brinell (1849–1925), a Swedish engineer who devised it. Brinell also invented the machine used to test the metals.

## Celsius

A scale for measuring temperature on which water boils at 100 degrees and freezes at zero degree, named for Anders Celsius (1701–1744), Swedish astronomer, who invented it.

Celsius was the first to propose a thermometer based on the centigrade scale, the most practical way to measure temperature. Today the Celsius scale has replaced most other scales for everyday all over the world.

## Charpy machine

A device for measuring the brittleness of materials by means of a pendulum drop hammer, named for its inventor, Augustin Charpy (1865–1945), a French engineer. Charpy was one of the three founders, all French, of the science of alloys.

## coulomb

A unit of electrical charge, named for Charles Augustin de Coulomb (1736–1806), French engineer and physicist.

## Fahrenheit

A scale for measuring temperature on which water boils at 212 degrees and freezes at 32 degrees, named for Gabriel Daniel Fahrenheit (1686–1736), a German-Dutch instrument maker, who devised it.

Fahrenheit's chief contribution was the substitution of mercury for alcohol in the tube, still used. He determined zero as the lowest temperature then obtainable (by mixing salt and ice), marked off the normal temperature of the human body as 96 degrees (2–3 degrees too low), and divided the intervening distance into individual degrees.

Fahrenheit's thermometer has been superseded by first Réaumur's (0 equal freezing, 80 equals boiling) and later Celsius (0 equals freezing, 100 equals boiling), and today Fahrenheit's is still used in conjunction with Celsius in Great Britain and the United States. Perhaps the newer scales lack the drama of "forty below!" and "over a hundred!"

## farad

A unit of electrical capacitance, named for Michael Faraday (1791–1867), virtual creator of the science of electricity.

Faraday built the first transformer, discovered how to generate electricity by means of magnets (which made possible commercial production and use of electricity), and carried out related experiments in electrochemistry, metallurgy, heat, acoustics, and numerous other fields. Many people consider Faraday, after Newton and Darwin, England's greatest scientific mind.

## faraday

A unit for measuring the quantity of electricity transferred in electrolysis, also named for Michael Faraday.

## gauss

A unit of magnetic induction, named for Karl F. Gauss (1777–1855), German mathematician and astronomer, who founded the mathematical theory of electricity. "Gauss's method" for calculating the orbits of celestial bodies is used today for tracking man-made satellites.

Gauss's mathematical brilliance first became evident at the age of three, when he called attention to some errors in his father's insurance-fund bookkeeping. At eighteen, while still a student at the University of Göttingen, he solved a geometrical problem that had been baffling mathematicians since Euclid's day. He is sometimes called one of the three greatest mathematicians in history, the other two being Archimedes and Newton.

## gilbert

A unit of magnetomotive force, named for William Gilbert (1544–1603), English physician and physicist, who founded the science of magnetism.

## henry

A unit of inductive resistance, named for Joseph Henry (1797–1878), American physicist. Henry, who was the first director of the Smithsonian Institution, designed an electric motor, instituted the weather-reporting system, and demonstrated an early version of the magnetic telegraph.

## hertz

A unit of frequency equal to one cycle per second, named for the German physicist Heinrich R. Hertz (1857–1894). Hertz's work in the field of electromagnets helped lay the foundation for the eventual development of radio and television.

## Johannson blocks

Gauges used for extremely fine measurement—to 1/100,000th of an inch—named for C. G. Johannson, Swedish engineer, who developed them.

## Jolly balance

A delicate spring balance used for the determination of density, named for Philipp von Jolly (1809–1884), a German physicist, who invented it.

## joule

An international unit of work or energy, named for English physicist James P. Joule (1818–1889), who first determined the mechanical equivalance of heat.

## kelvin scale

A scale for measuring temperature in which 0 equals absolute zero or total absence of heat (−273.6 C or −459.69 F) and water freezes at 273 degrees and boils at 373 degrees, named for William Thomson, Lord Kelvin (1824–1907), British physicist.

Kelvin, who worked in the field of thermodynamics and electrodynamics, produced studies and inventions in a number of different fields. He was knighted in 1866 for his contributions toward the laying of the transatlantic cable and thirty years later was made a peer.

## lambert

A unit of brightness, named for Johann Heinrich Lambert (1728–1777), German physicist and mathematician, whose studies were chiefly in the fields of light, color, and heat.

## langley

A unit of solar radiation, named for Samuel P. Langley (1834–1906), American astronomer and airplane designer, who invented the bolometer for measuring heat radiation.

An early experimenter in heavier-than-air flying machines, Langley in 1896 sent up a motor-driven plane that stayed aloft for 3,000 feet. He was never able to design a machine capable of carrying a man, but his example was an inspiration for Orville and Wilbur Wright, who were.

## Mach number

A number used in measuring the speed of an object, such as an airplane, in comparison to the speed of sound, named for Ernst Mach (1838–1916), Austrian physicist. Mach's field was investigation of the physiology and psychology of the senses.

A Mach number under 1 (0.50) indicates a subsonic speed, a number over 1 (1.5,5, 7.2, etc.) indicates a supersonic speed—that is, one faster than the speed of sound.

## McLeod gauge

A device for measuring the pressure of gas, named for Herbert McLeod, an English chemist, who invented it.

## Mohs scale

A scale for measuring the hardness of minerals, named for Friedrich Mohs (1773–1839), a German mineralogist, who devised it. According to Mohs's system, talc has the hardness of 1 and diamond of 10, and other minerals lie at various points along the scale in between.

## newton

A unit of force equal to an acceleration of one meter per second, named for the great English mathematician Sir Isaac Newton (1642–1727).

Newton is best known, of course, for the discovery of gravitational force, but he also invented calculus, calculated the pull between the earth and the moon, and originated theories of light and optics. He is considered one of the most brilliant minds of all time, and many of his theories of time and space were not seriously challenged until Albert Einstein produced the theory of relativity.

## oersted

A unit of magnetic intensity, named for Hans Christian Oersted (1777–1851), Danish chemist and physicist, who discovered the principle of electromagnetism.

## ohm

A unit of electrical resistance, named for Georg Simon Ohm (1787–1854), German physicist, who discovered the relationship among the intensity of an electrical current, the force behind it, and the resistance of a circuit.

## Pitot tube

A device for measuring the velocity of flowing fluids and moving ships, named for Henri Pitot (1695–1771), a French physicist, who invented it. Pitot also designed the aqueduct at Montpellier, France.

## Réaumur scale

A scale for measuring temperature in which water freezes at 0 degrees and boils at 80 degrees, named for its deviser, René de Réaumur (1683–1757).

## Richter scale

A system for measuring the magnitude of a seismic disturbance, named for Charles R. Richter (b. 1900), American seismologist, who devised it. On the Richter scale, which runs from 1 to 10, 1.5 represents the smallest earthquake that can be felt, 4.5 a quake that does slight damage, and 8.3 (as in San Francisco, April 18–19, 1906) a devastating upheaval.


## roentgen

An international unit of X-ray radiation, named for the discoverer of X-rays, Wilhelm Conrad Roentgen (1845–1923), a German physicist. Roentgen first discovered the properties of X-rays, in 1894, while he was experimenting with the conduction of electricity through gases. In 1901, he received the first Nobel prize to be awarded in the field of physics.


## rutherford

A unit for measuring the strength of radioactive emissions, named for Ernest Lord Rutherford (1876–1937), a British nuclear physicist, who did his principal work on the radioactive disintegration of elements.


## sabin

A unit of acoustic absorption, named for Wallace C. Sabine (1868–1919), American physicist, renowned for his research in acoustics. He designed the acoustical system of Symphony Hall, Boston.


## tesla

In the International Measurement System, a unit of magnetic-flux density, named in honor of Nikola Tesla (1856–1943), a Yugoslav-American electrician and inventor. Among other things, Tesla invented the alternating motor.


## torr

A unit of pressure, named for Evangelista Torricelli (1608–1647), who invented the mercury barometer. Torricelli, who had served as a secretary to Galileo in his declining years, after his death was appointed to fill his place as court mathematician to the grand duke of Tuscany.

## venturi

A tube constructed to measure the velocity and pressure of fluids, named for G. B. Venturi (1746–1822), who was the first to work on its principles.

## vernier

A small movable scale that attaches to a larger one to obtain more accurate measurements, named for Pierre Vernier (1584–1638), a French mathematician, who invented it.

## volt

A unit of electromotive force, named in 1881 for Count Alessandro Volta (1745–1827), Italian physicist and pioneer investigator of the phenomenon of electricity.

## watt

A unit of power equal to one absolute joule per hour, named for James Watt (1736–1819), a Scots engineer, who greatly improved the early steam engine. He and his partner, Matthew Boulton, coined the term "horsepower."

## weber

A unit of magnetic flux, named for Wilhelm E. Weber (1804–1891), German physicist, who did important work on electromagnetism.

# · 15 ·

# Belligerence: From Name-Calling to Weaponry

Earthly existence is not, unfortunately, always wine and roses. Our language contains many words and expressions that denote name-calling, outrageous actions, places and situations of destruction, and instruments of war. Here are some of them.

## NAME CALLING . . .

### assassin

Someone who murders a public figure for political or other public reasons, named for the Hashshashin of Persia, a fanatical Muslim sect founded in the eleventh century and reputedly habituated to murdering unbelievers while under the influence of hashish.

### Benedict Arnold

A traitor to a cause, named for Major General Benedict Arnold (1741–1801), American army officer, who plotted with the British to surrender the defenses at West Point in exchange for money and a King's commission.

Arnold, a genuine hero in the early months of the Revolutionary War, twice wounded and credited with a major share of the crucial American victory at Saratoga (September–October, 1777), felt slighted

291

by Congress. In debt and offended by the American treaty with France, he did an about-face and offered his services to the British, only to be thwarted at the last moment by the accidental capture of Major John André, his co-conspirator. He fled to the British and eventually to England. For this spectacular attempt at treason, he was paid £6,525 plus a pension for his wife.

## billingsgate

Loud, coarse, abusive language, named for Billingsgate fish market in London, where fishmongers were famous for their foul mouths.

Billingsgate itself, which is believed to have existed on this same spot since the ninth century, may have taken its name from Belin, a king of the ancient Britons. "Gate" is derived from an old Germanic word for "street."

## blarney

Charming cajolerie, smooth talk, named for the famed Blarney Stone, set in the parapet of Blarney Castle, County Cork, Eire. Legend maintains that anyone who kisses the Blarney Stone—not easy to do, since one must lean backward over a 150-foot drop, head upside down, to manage it—will be granted the gift of a persuasive tongue.

## Boeotian

A thickheaded boor, named for the region of Greece north and west of Attica (capital Thebes), whose inhabitants were regarded by other Greeks as dull and stupid.

## bohunk

A pejorative term for an unskilled worker of foreign origin, particularly from eastern Europe, named for a combination of "Bohemian" and "Hungarian."

## Bronx cheer

The raspberry, a vulgar sound made by extending the tongue between protruded lips and blowing, named for the borough of the Bronx, New York City, whose inhabitants are traditionally quick to show displeasure.

## bunk

Nonsense, meaningless rhetoric, named for Buncombe County, North Carolina. In 1820, during the House debate on the all-important Missouri Compromise, Congressman Felix Walker insisted on interjecting an irrelevant speech praising his home county. When other members objected, Walker replied blandly, "I am speaking to Buncombe."

## cain

Uproar, disturbance, named for the biblical Cain, who murdered his brother Abel in a fit of jealousy.

## diddle

To cheat or hoax someone, named for the fictional Jeremy Diddler in James Kenney's 1803 farce, *Raising the Wind*. Jeremy was perpetually borrowing small sums of money and never returning them.

## guinea pig

A small thick-bodied rodent, widely used in research because of its rapid breeding habits, named "guinea" (an African region) by mistake for Guiana (a South American region), where it comes from. By extension, human beings used for experimental purposes—with or without their own knowledge and consent—are also called guinea pigs.

## Hobson's choice

No choice at all, named for Thomas Hobson, seventeenth-century

English livery-stable proprietor, who forced every customer to take the horse that stood nearest to the door.

## jabberwocky

Meaningless speech, gibberish, usually used contemptuously, named for Lewis Carroll's nonsense poem "Jabberwocky" in *Through the Looking Glass.*

## jeremiad

A gloomy tirade, named for the biblical Jeremiah (640–570 B.C.) who predicted the decline of the land of Judah. The five-chapter book called The Lamentations of Jeremiah is one long tale of woe.

## Job's comforter

Someone who, while professing to sympathize with another's troubles, adds to them by tactless remarks, named for the biblical Job whose friends offered nothing but harsh comments.

> Then Job answered [Eliphaz the Temanite] and said, I have heard many such things; miserable comforters are ye all. (Job 16:1–2)

## Jonah

A jinx, one who brings bad luck, especially to a ship at sea, named for the biblical Jonah, whose disobedience to God brought down a severe storm on the ship he was traveling in. Ordered by God to visit Ninevah and denounce the sins of the inhabitants, the prophet refused and instead hurried off by sea in the opposite direction. God then created a tumultous storm that endangered all on board. Seeing what was happening, Jonah said to the sailors:

> Take me up and cast me forth into the sea: so shall the sea be calm unto you. . . . So they took up Jonah and cast him forth into the sea: and the sea ceased from her raging. (Jonah 1:12–15)

## Judas

A traitor, someone who pretends friendship and then betrays, named for Judas Iscariot, who betrayed Jesus with a kiss:

> Now he that betrayed him gave them a sign, saying, Whomsoever I shall kiss, the same is he: hold him fast. And forthwith he came to Jesus, and said, Hail, master; and kissed him. (Matthew 26:48–49)

## Jukes and Kallikaks

Degenerate oafs, socially, intellectually, and morally inferior people, named for the fictionalized names of families used in two classic psychosocial studies: *The Jukes, a Study in Crime, Pauperism, Disease, and Heredity* (1877) by Richard L. Dugdale and *The Kallikak Family* (1912) by Henry Herbert Goddard.

*The Jukes* is the story of a New York State family, the descendants of two brothers who married two sisters; out of 1,200 members of this one family, 140 were imprisoned for crimes and 280 were paupers, dependent on public support. The Kallikaks were two New Jersey families, the descendants of a Revolutionary soldier. One family, his children by a feebleminded woman, produced a high percentage of criminals and morons (a term Goddard invented), whereas the same man's descendants by the normal woman he married were bright, honest, and upright.

Both writers concluded from their studies that feeblemindedness, crime, and antisocial behavior are inherited. Modern authorities, however, point out that neither scholar made sufficient allowance for environmental and social factors.

## Madison Avenue

An adjective meaning "characteristic of the advertising and publicity businesses," named for Madison Avenue in New York City, where many advertising agencies have their offices. The term is sometimes, but not always, used disparagingly.

## mud

Anathema, someone beyond the pale, named for Dr. Samuel Alexander Mudd, who was given a life sentence for setting the broken leg of Presidential assassin John Wilkes Booth. Mudd was later pardoned by President Andrew Johnson for helping end a prison epidemic of yellow fever.

## plug-ugly

A thug, a lout of low intelligence, great muscular strength, and mean disposition, named for the Plug Uglies, a gang of street ruffians who prowled the alleys of New York City in the 1830's. The gang, chiefly Irish, wore plug hats (stiff top hats shaped like a plug, with the flat top slightly larger in circumference than the band) and were sometimes used for political strong-arm tactics.

## tawdry

Cheap or gaudy-looking, named for Saint Audrey, or Etheldreda (630–679), East Anglian princess, who—in spite of being an abbess and the founder of a double monastery—liked to wear necklaces. It is said that this weakness was the cause of her being afflicted with a throat tumor, from which she died.

## Teddy boy

A foppish British hoodlum of the 1950's, who affected Edwardian costume as part of his public "image," named for "King Teddy," the affectionate nickname bestowed on the popular monarch, Edward VII.

## thug

A brute, a bully, a professional strong-arm man or someone whose natural disposition is toward roughing up those who are weaker than he, named for the Thugs, a group of professional robbers and murderers who flourished in seventeenth- and eighteenth-century India.

The Thugs, who practiced thuggee (robbery and murder by strangulation) were originally followers of Kali, the goddess of destruction. They killed ritualistically by means of a yard of cotton cloth, often having stupefied their victims first with drugs, and then would take whatever belongings the dead man left behind. The poor, the low caste, the crippled, and women were supposedly immune, but the Thugs often killed them anyway, in order not to leave witnesses behind. Finally in 1828 the British colonial authorities mounted a campaign against them and by midcentury had wiped them out.

## Typhoid Mary

An unwitting harbinger of trouble, named for Typhoid Mary Mallon, a turn-of-the-century cook in New York City, who was the first recognized typhoid carrier—someone who is immune to the disease himself but carries it about infecting others. It is estimated that during the thirty-one years Mary Mallon was at large she caused at least ten outbreaks of fever—fifty-one cases and three deaths. Today known carriers are carefully overseen by public-health officials to prevent the spread of infection.

# OUTRAGEOUS ACTIONS . . .

## babel

A confusion of sounds, usually caused by several people speaking at the same time, named for the Biblical tower of Babel. The descendants of Noah gathered at a plain in the land of Shinar and decided to build a tower that would reach the heavens. Such audacity angered God, who punished them:

> Therefore is the name of it called Babel [gate of God];
> because of the Lord did there confound the language of all
> the earth [that is, made all languages mutually unintelligible]: and from thence did the Lord scatter them abroad.
> (Genesis 11:9)

## bacchanalia

A wild, drunken celebration, named for Bacchus, the Roman god of wine and vines, whose followers indulged in ritual orgies of drinking and revelry, usually on the occasion of opening the new wine casks each season. In 186 B.C. the Senate put an end to them.

## burke

To strangle someone or to suppress a matter quietly and clandestinely, named for William Burke (1792–1829), Scots murderer, who with his partner William Hare strangled guests at Hare's sordid tavern in order to sell their cadavers to a local anatomist. They earned from £7 to £14 apiece for their "merchandise."

## Jim Crow

Pejorative term for laws, regulations, or private actions that discriminate against black people, particularly those that enforce segregation, named for the anonymous song "Jump, Jim Crow."

In 1830, Thomas "Daddy" Rice introduced the song (which he had seen an old Negro stablehand perform) to theatrical audiences, thus founding the immensely popular black-faced minstrel shows. Blacks, who considered both the song and blackface performance insulting. applied the term "Jim Crow" to the system of segregation itself.

## lynch

To hang someone without trial, on suspicion of having committed rape or murder, usually by mob action, named probably for Colonel Charles Lynch (1736–1796), judge of an unauthorized court established in Virginia during the Revolution.

Originally "Lynch's law" meant flogging, but in the post–Civil War period it came to signify execution, most often of Negroes. Between 1882 and 1951, no fewer than 4,730 people were lynched in the United States—3,437 blacks and 1,293 whites.

## Munich

A feeble cave-in to the demands of a bully, named for the city of Munich, Bavaria, West Germany, where in September, 1938, a four-power conference (England, France, Germany, and Italy) meekly abandoned Czechoslovakia's territorial rights to Adolf Hitler.

The history of Naziism has strong ties to Munich. It was here that the party was born in 1920 and that Hitler tried to take over the German government by force in the comic-opera Beer Hall Putsch of 1923. It was also the site of an unsuccessful revolt against Hitler by university students in 1942.

## Pearl Harbor

A sudden sneak attack, named for the U.S. Naval Base at Pearl Harbor, Hawaii, which on December 7, 1941, was attacked without warning, while the two nations were at peace, by air and naval forces of Japan.

The results of Pearl Harbor were devastating: 2,500 Americans killed, nineteen ships sunk or badly damaged, 180 American aircraft destroyed. But the primary target of the raid, the Navy's fleet of aircraft carriers, was at sea that weekend and escaped.

## shanghai

To take someone forcibly where he does not want to go, named for Shanghai, China, since crews for China-bound ships were often obtained by strong-arm methods. The usual technique was to prowl waterfront taverns on the lookout for likely prospects, get them drunk (or drug them), and then drag them aboard. By the time they came to themselves, the vessel would be far at sea, and they would have no choice but to help work the sails.

## slavery

Bondage, the state of being under the control of another's will, named for the Slavs of eastern Europe and the Balkans, who in the Dark Ages were often raided by their more powerful neighbors and enslaved.

Slavery is thousands of years old, being accepted by societies of all degrees of sophistication. It was introduced into North America in 1619, when a Dutch man-of-war stopped by at Jamestown and traded twenty Africans for needed supplies, and it lasted until the end of the American Civil War in 1865. The last European-populated country to abolish slavery was Brazil, which did so between 1871 and 1888.

## Trojan horse

An agent of the enemy in one's midst, who by sabotage or espionage will undermine one's course of action, named for the device whereby the Greeks defeated the Trojans.

After ten years of struggle and the deaths of many Greek heroes, the Greeks had not been able to take the city of Troy. Therefore, at the suggest of the wily Odysseus (Ulysses), they built a huge wooden horse, filled it secretly with armed men, and left it on the shore ostensibly as an offering to Athena. Then they pretended to sail away. When the Trojans had dragged the horse inside, having broken down part of their walls to do so, the hidden men emerged, the rest of the Greeks returned, and Troy fell.

# PLACES OF EVIL MEMORY . . .

## Babylon

A large city regarded as wealthy and wicked, named for the ancient capital of Babylonia, which seemed to the austere nomadic pastoral peoples a perfect den of iniquity.

## bedlam

Uproar, confusion, tumult, named for the hospital of St. Mary of Bethlehem (corrupted to Bedlam), London, since 1402 an asylum for the insane. In the seventeenth and eighteenth centuries, it was a popular amusement to visit the hospital and laugh at the antics of the lunatics, and from the noise they made came the popular usage of "bedlam."

## black hole

A place of close and noisome confinement, named for the Black Hole of Calcutta, a small punishment cell belonging to the British East India Company, where during the night of June 20–21, 1757, 146 Europeans were supposedly confined by the ruler of Bengal. According to the story, which is of doubtful authenticity, 123 of the prisoners suffocated before morning. Modern research has revised those figures somewhat, and it is now believed that no more than forty persons were confined in the cell, of whom perhaps fifteen may have died.

It was customary in the British Army, at least in the eighteenth century, to confine soldiers guilty of minor offenses to a small dark cell for a day or two (instead of flogging them), and this was called a black hole.

## Coventry

A state or place of ostracism, named for the city of Coventry in Warwickshire, England, to which royalist prisoners were sent during the English Civil War.

## Gehenna

A place of great suffering, a hell, from the biblical Ge' Hinnom (valley of Hinnom) outside ancient Jerusalem, where fires burned continuously to disinfect garbage and dispose of the bodies of criminals and animals. The Old Testament refers to Gehenna as a place where idol worshipers sacrificed their children to the god Moloch, and the kings Ahaz and Menasseh are condemned by the author of II Chronicles for offering incense in Hinnom to the heathen deities. Hence, "Gehenna" came to be the name of a place of horrors and abominations.

Other major religions have their forms of "hell," too. Buddhists have seven "hot hells." The Hindu Rig Veda refers to a bottomless pit for women who are faithless and men who are false. Muslims have seven hells to correspond with their seven heavens, and the New Testament speaks of sinners thrown into a lake of fire.

## golgotha

A cemetary, sometimes a place of suffering, named for the hill of Golgotha near ancient Jerusalem on which Jesus was crucified. ("Calvary" is the English form of "Golgotha.") *Golgotha*, an Aramaic word meaning "place of the skull," refers either to the skull-like shape of the hill or to the skulls that were found around it.

## hades

A mild word for "hell," often used as a substitute for it in polite speech, named for the Greek underworld and its ruling god, Hades. Actually, the Greeks referred to the place in the genitive, Hades', much as modern people refer to their friends' places of residence: "I'm going over to Henry's . . . I stopped by at Sally's. . . ."

Hades was surrounded by five rivers, of which the most famous were Acheron and Styx. To reach it, the dead had to be ferried across by Charon, a grumbling old boatman, who had the right to demand a fare of one obol per soul. (The coin was placed in the dead person's mouth.) The gates of Hades were guarded by the fierce three-headed dog Cerberus, and once the dead man had passed him, he drank from the sixth river of the underworld, the Lethe, which caused him to forget his earthly existence. If he had led a blameless life, he then went to eternal bliss in the beautiful meadows of Elysium; if he had not, he was consigned to Tartarus, where he might or might not be punished.

## Siberia

A desolate place of exile, at the end of nowhere, named for the vast region of eastern Russia, to which political troublemakers and criminals were sent. Large areas of Siberia are above the Arctic Circle, and winter temperatures are frequently recorded as low as −40 degrees Fahrenheit.

## Sodom and Gomorrah

A place where vice and corruption abound, often used with humorous exaggeration, named for two cities of the ancient Near East whose exact location is unknown.

Then the Lord rained upon Sodom and upon Gomorrah brimstone and fire from the Lord out of heaven; And he overthrew those cities, and that which grew upon the ground. (Genesis 19:24–25)

## Stygian

Gloomy, cavernous, dark, named for the mythological River Styx, which souls had to cross to reach Hades.

## tophet

Another mild word for "hell," named for the shrine near Gehenna, where child sacrifices were made to the gods Moloch and Baal.

And they have built the high places of Tophet, which is in the valley of the son of Hinnom, to burn their sons and daughters in the fire; which I commanded them not. . . . (Jeremiah 7:31)

# CALAMITOUS EVENTS . . .

## Armageddon

A climactic, widespread fight to the death, named for the ancient mountainous region of Har-Megiddon on the plain of Esdraelon, where the New Testament predicts a final battle between the armies of good and evil:

For they are the spirits of devils, working miracles, which go forth unto the kings of the earth and of the whole world, to gather them to the battle of that great day of God Almighty . . . And he gathered them together into a place called in the Hebrew tongue Armageddon. (Revelation 16:14–16)

## Cadmean victory

A victory achieved at ruinous cost, named for the mythological

Cadmus, who sowed dragon's teeth, from which sprang an army of warriors who fought until all but five had been killed.

## Calvary

A grueling experience, an ordeal, named for the hill near Jerusalem (see *Golgotha*) where Jesus suffered crucifixion.

And when they were come to the place, which is called Calvary, there they crucified him, and the malefactors, one on the right hand, and the other on the left. (Luke 24:33)

## Donnybrook

A free-for-all brawl, named for Donnybrook Fair, founded in Donnybrook, Eire (a suburb of Dublin), in 1204. The fair became so notorious for the scrapping that took place there that it was abolished in 1855.

## juggernaut

A massive and unstoppable force that rolls down relentlessly on anything or anybody that stands in its way, named for Jagannath, "Lord of the World," a title of Vishnu, one of the Hindu gods.

In the seacoast town of Puri, Orissa, India, there is an annual religious procession, in which the statue of the god is carried on an elaborate cart with huge wheels. Pilgrims drag the cart through sand from one site to another, a feat which takes several days to accomplish. There was a mistaken belief among Europeans that great numbers of people were regularly crushed under the wheels—a delusion apparently stemming from the fact that on rare occasions someone does commit suicide by flinging himself into the path of the car of Jagannath.

## nemesis

Greek goddess of due proportion. Nemesis, the daughter of Night, punished people for presumption and boastfulness.

## pandemonium

A state of uproar and wild confusion, named for Pandaemonium ("place of all demons"), the capital of Hell in John Milton's *Paradise Lost*.

## Pandora's box

Something that produces a profusion of troubles and problems, named for the mythical Pandora ("all gifts"). Zeus bestowed on the girl as her dowry a sealed box and warned her not to open it. Consumed by curiosity, however, she unsealed the box, and out flew all the troubles of mankind. The only thing that remained in the box was Elpis, Hope.

## panic

A sudden overpowering fright, which often causes its victim to behave irrationally, named for the mythical Pan, god of shepherds and woods, who was believed by the ancient Greeks to cause it.

Panic is nearly always the result of an *unexpected* disaster, and in crowds it is infectious. In fires, panic-stricken crowds have trampled down others in their rush to escape, causing pileups at entranceways that prevent the very exodus they are trying to achieve. In other emergencies, panic causes people to freeze and refuse to move, even when it is essential that they do something to help themselves.

In the economic sense, a panic ensues when lack of confidence in financial institutions and business sends people rushing to withdraw money from banks and securities in which it is invested.

## Paris garden

A scene of uproar and tumult, named for the Paris Garden, Southwark, London, where crowds surged to watch the brutal sports of bear and bull baiting and prizefighting. In Shakespeare's *Henry VIII*, a porter reprimands men who make a racket in the palace yard:

> You'll leave your noise anon, you rascals: do you take the court for Paris-garden?

## Pyrrhic victory

Success achieved at the price of ruinous losses, named for Pyrrhus (319–272 B.C.), king of Epirus, a region of ancient Greece that is now partly Greece and partly Albania. Pyrrhus, a great soldier, went to the assistance of Tarentum in its struggles to resist the domination of Rome, and twice defeated the Romans. After the second battle, at which his losses had been heavy, he was congratulated on the victory and replied, "Another such victory over the Romans, and we are utterly undone."

## Roman holiday

A period of enjoyment at the expense of others, named for the Roman method of celebrating great events with gladiatorial contests and circuses in which people fought animals or animals fought one another. During one four-month period in A.D. 107, ten thousand gladiators were sent into the arena by the Emperor Trajan—and Trajan is considered by historians one of the "good" emperors.

## Sword of Damocles

A calamity that may occur at any time, often from slight causes, named for Damocles the Syracusan. Damocles, a friend of Dionysius the Elder (430–367 B.C.), ruler of Syracuse, commented to his friend that he was a fortunate man. To demonstrate the uncertainty and anxiety of a ruler's life, Dionysius invited Damocles to a banquet and then seated him at the table under a dangling sword, hanging by a single thread.

## Waterloo

A calamitous or final defeat, named for the dramatic battle fought at Waterloo, just south of Brussels, on June 18, 1815, between Napoleon Bonaparte and Allied forces under Blücher and Wellington. For Napoleon it was the end of his career. Taken prisoner, he was sent to St. Helena Island, in the South Atlantic, where he died six years later of stomach cancer.

# INSTRUMENTS OF WAR AND DESTRUCTION . . .

## bangalore torpedo

An explosive device in the form of a long metal tube containing explosive materials and a firing mechanism, named for Bangalore, Mysore, India, where the British maintained a military station. It is used chiefly for clearing a path through barbed-wire entanglements.

## Big Bertha

Any large, ungainly apparatus, but particularly a mortar of large bore (420 mm) and long range used by the Germans in World War I, named for Frau Bertha Krupp von Bohlen and Halbach (1886–1957), owner of the Krupp works and great-granddaughter of its founder.

Big Bertha, though used devastatingly in Belgium and at Verdun, was *not* the long-range cannon with which the Germans bombarded Paris from seventy-five miles away.

## bilbo

An iron bar with shackles used as fetters (leg irons) especially on board ship, named for Bilboa, Spain, where the device originated.

## Bofors gun

A rapid-fire, double-barreled antiaircraft gun, named for the Bofors munition works in Sweden, where it is made.

## Bowie knife

A single-edged hunting knife with a slightly curved tip, and a guarded haft, ten to fifteen inches long, named for James Bowie (1799–1836), who popularized it. The knife was probably designed by Jim's older brother Rezin, who supposedly lost three fingers using a guardless knife to cut up a wild steer.

The chief use of the Bowie knife seems to have been in frontier brawls. Jim Bowie himself is said to have used it successfully in a notorious mass duel fought at Natchez, Mississippi, on September 19, 1827.


## Bren gun

A gas-operated, shoulder-firing machine gun, named for the cities where it was manufactured—*Br*no, Czechoslovakia, and *En*field in Middlesex, England.


## Browning automatic

Any of several different machine guns or machine rifles, rapid-fire, either air- or water-cooled, named for John Moses Browning, an American gunsmith (1855–1926), who developed the first one.


## carronade

A powerful, short-range naval gun, named for Carron in Stirlingshire, Scotland, where it was cast. The carronade, originally called the Smasher, operated on a relatively light powder charge and had poor power to penetrate, but if a naval officer could lay his ship alongside the enemy's, it would blow an enormous hole in its side.


## chassepot

A bolt-action rifle, named for its inventor, Antoine A. Chassepot (1833–1905). It was used by the French army in 1866.


## cheval-de-frise ("horse of Friesland")

A military device, consisting of a number of iron-tipped stakes arranged to project in bristling fashion, used to block up a breach in a system of defenses, named for a province of the Netherlands, where it was first produced. Chevaux-de-frise were the forerunners of barbed wire.

## Colt

A revolver, usually .45 caliber, named for Samuel Colt (1814–1862), who invented the first practical multishot firearm.

The original six-shooter was popularized by the Mexican War, and it continued to be a favorite with cowhands and settlers in the raw West. It is sometimes called the Gun That Won the West, and there is a saying among Texans: "Sam Houston made us free, and Sam Colt made us equal."

## derringer

A short-barreled pocket pistol, named for its designer, Henry Deringer (1786–1868), a Philadelphia gunsmith.

Because they were small and designed to be carried concealed, derringers had a somewhat dubious reputation. John Wilkes Booth used a derringer to assassinate President Lincoln.

## dumdum

A soft-nosed bullet that expands when it strikes a hard surface—like human bones—causing a large and jagged wound, named for Dum Dum, a suburb of Calcutta, India, where the British had an arsenal. The British Army used the dumdum on hill tribesmen, whose impetuous charges could not be stopped by conventional bullets.

Because of their devastating effect, dumdums were outlawed by the 1898 Hague Convention.

## Enfield rifle

The standard rifle issued to men of the British Army since the Crimean War, named for Enfield Lock, royal small-arms factory in Enfield, Middlesex, England.

An American inventor, James P. Lee (1831–1904), designed a version of the Enfield that was magazine fed and made to hold a knife bayonet, and this is known as the Lee-Enfield.

## Garand

The U.S. Army's M-1 semiautomatic rifle, widely used by infantrymen in World War II, named for its designer, John Cantius Garand (b. 1888).

## gatling gun

A crank-operated machine gun, consisting of a cluster of barrels (usually ten), named for its inventor, Richard Jordon Gatling (1818–1903). Although the gun was patented in 1862, the U.S. Army did not accept it until 1866, so it missed out on the Civil War. Thereafter it was used in every war for the next half century.

## "Geronimo!"

Battle cry or inspiriting yell uttered by American paratroopers at the moment of the jump, named for Apache warrior Geronimo (1829–1909), whose raids caused considerable trouble in the 1880's. It is not known why Geronimo's name was turned into a paratrooper's shout.

## Greek fire

A flammable mixture of naphtha, niter, and sulfur (the exact composition is unknown) used by the Greeks of Byzantium to burn the ships of their enemies. The formula, perfected in Constantinople by a Syrian refugee named Callinicus, could not be extinguished by water. It was projected through copper tubes.

## guillotine

A device for lopping off the heads of condemned persons quickly and (it was hoped) painlessly, named for the man who proposed its adoption by the French National Assembly in 1789, Dr. Joseph I. Guillotin (1738–1814). The proposal was an act of humanity.

Before the guillotine, beheading had been a grisly business, often clumsily mismanaged, the headsman taking three or four whacks to finish the job. Ironically, it was a privilege to die by beheading, reserved for the aristocracy; common people were normally hanged.

With the help of Monsieur de Paris (official executioner for the national government), Charles-Henri Sanson, Guillotin devised the instrument that goes by his name. According to one story, the plans for the first guillotine were shown to Louis XVI, and the king, himself a skilled locksmith and clock repairer, pointed out that the crescent blade Sanson and Guillotin wanted was the wrong shape. It should be triangular, he said, with an edge beveled like a scythe. The change was made, and a few months later Louis' own head fell beneath a triangular blade.

Guillotin did not enjoy having this instrument of execution named after him and never witnessed it in use. Yet when he walked in the streets of Paris, passersby jeered at him and made mocking chops on the backs of their necks. After his death, his children petitioned the French government to call La Machine by some other name. The government refused but granted them permission to change theirs.

## lewisite

A geranium-smelling liquid used to create an extremely poisonous gas, named for the American chemist who compounded it, Winford Lee Lewis (1878–1943). Lewisite, which is similar to mustard gas in that it raises blisters, was developed during World War I but never used.

## Maham tower

A crude wooden stand, higher than the palisades of a frontier fort, from which sharpshooters could pick off members of a defending garrison, named for Colonel Hezekiah Maham of South Carolina. During the American Revolution, Maham towers enabled Patriot troops to force the surrender of Loyalist-held strongholds without the use of artillery or entrenching tools.

## Martello tower

A circular stone fort, named for the fortification at Cape Mortella, Corsica, which was captured by the British in 1794.

## Mata Hari

A seductive female, particularly one who attempts to pry secrets from her victims, often used humorously, named for the stage name of Gertrud Margarete Zelle (1876–1917), German spy in World War I.

In 1903, the divorced mother of two, a Dutch subject, went to Paris to become a professional entertainer. She had some success as an erotic dancer, presenting herself under the name "Mata Hari" as a native of India, and made many contacts among government people. The Germans sent her to spy school, after which she returned to Paris, and when war broke out, she began sending secret information to them (especially about the flying services). The French knew of her activities, but couldn't prove anything against her until 1917. Then finally Mata Hari was tried and condemned. She was executed by a firing squad at Vincennes, October 15, 1917.

## Mauser

A repeating pistol or rifle, named for its inventor, Peter Paul Mauser (1838–1914), a gunsmith at the royal armory in Oberndorf, Wurttemberg-Hohenzollern, West Germany.

Mauser's first weapon, designed with the help of his brother Wilhelm (1834–1882), was a needle gun—a military weapon with a needlelike firing pin, which enjoyed a brief popularity in midnineteenth-century Europe. Later the brothers purchased the armory to go into business for themselves, and there they invented the Mauser magazine rifle in 1897. It became the standard German arm in World War I and II.

## Maxim gun

The world's first machine gun, named for its inventor, American-born British engineer Sir Hiram Maxim.

A versatile inventor, Sir Hiram held 122 patents in the United States and 149 in Great Britain, including those for an improved curling iron, an improved incandescent lamp, smokeless powder, an aerial torpedo gun, an automatic-sprinkler fire extinguisher—and an improved mouse-trap.

His son, Hiram Percy Maxim, was likewise an inventor, especially of electrical apparatus and devices to improve the performance of automobiles. He developed the auto muffler and from there went on to his best-known invention, the Maxim silencer for guns.

## Minie ball

A cone-headed bullet used in nineteenth-century muzzle-loading rifles, named for its inventor Claude Étienne Minié (1804–1879), a French army officer. The "minny ball" was the standard military bullet used by both sides throughout the American Civil War.

## Molotov cocktail

A homemade fire bomb, consisting of a bottle half-filled with gasoline or other flammable liquid and a rag wick, named for Vyacheslav Mikhailovich Molotov (b. 1890), Soviet foreign minister. The wick is lighted and the bottle thrown; it explodes on contact and spreads fire.

The Finns, attacked by the Russians in 1940, used this crude weapon against them and gave it its ironic name, bestowed in memory of the nonaggression pact between Soviet Russia and Nazi Germany (which left Russia free to attack her neighbor), negotiated by Molotov.

## pavis

A large, free-standing shield set up by attackers to protect crossbow-men during a siege, named for Pavia, Italy.

## Quaker gun

A dummy gun, usually a tree trunk, mounted in a vacant embrasure to fool an enemy, named for the Quakers (the Society of Friends), who were renowned pacifists. The Confederates frequently used this device to make the Federals think their fortifications were better armed than they were.

## shillelagh

An Irishman's club, usually knobby, made of either oak or blackthorn wood, named for the town of Shillelagh, County Wicklow, Eire, famous for its oaks.

## Springfield rifle

The standard U.S. Army infantry rifle from 1868 through World War I, named for Springfield, Massachusetts, where the United States maintains an armory.

## Sten gun

A lightweight British machine gun, capable of firing 550 rounds per minute, named for an acronym of its designers' initials: Major *S*heppard, Mr. *T*urpin, plus *En*gland.

## tommy gun

The Thompson submachine gun, a light automatic weapon named for John Taliaferro Thompson (1860–1940), American army officer, who invented it. The tommy gun is best known, however, not for its military uses but for the many gangland rubouts effected with it, particularly during the 1920's.

## Valhalla

A place of honor, usually for the heroic dead, named for the hall of Odin in Norse mythology, to which the souls of heroes fallen in battle were carried, for an eternity of drinking and rejoicing. The Valkyries, "Choosers of the Slain," hovered over every field of battle to determine which men should die and which live, and to carry those who died nobly to Valhalla.

## Winchester

A repeating rifle, an improved model based on the Henry and Spencer repeating rifles of Civil War fame, named for the man who bought up the patents and sponsored the development of the new composite, Oliver Fisher Winchester (1810–1880).

The Winchester rifle was as much a part of the Old West as the Colt revolver. At the Fetterman massacre in 1866, it is said that two civilians, armed with Winchester repeaters, killed as many Indians as the eighty soldiers with them.